Chapters in
Anglo-Portuguese Relations

EDITED BY

EDGAR PRESTAGE, M.A., D.Litt.
Camoens Professor in the University of London

GREENWOOD PRESS, PUBLISHERS
WESTPORT, CONNECTICUT

Originally published in 1935
by Voss and Michael, Ltd., Watford

First Greenwood Reprinting 1971

Library of Congress Catalogue Card Number 73-109826

SBN 8371-4317-9

Printed in the United States of America

CONTENTS

v

PREFACE

The first five of the following Chapters consist of as many Public Lectures which were delivered in the Portuguese Department at King's College, London, in May, 1934. There was a sixth Lecture entitled *The Period of Anglo-Portuguese Hostility*, 1530–1584 by Dr. J. A. Williamson, but he was unable to reduce it to writing owing to the many calls on his time. The substance of it will, however, be found in my paper, *The Anglo-Portuguese Alliance*, read before the Royal Historical Society in November, 1933, and printed in Vol. XVII of its *Transactions* (1934). Chapter 6 contains a Lecture I gave at King's College in March, 1935, and it is included at the suggestion of His Excellency the Portuguese Ambassador, Dr. Ruy Ulrich, who was kind enough to recommend his government to subsidise the publication of the book. The Contributors desire to express their gratitude to him for this favour and also to Professor David Lopes, who asked that part of the money voted by the Junta de Educação Nacional for the foundation of an Historical Institute under his presidency should be used for the book. Their thanks are also due to Dr. Francisco de Paula Leite Pinto, General Secretary of the Junta, for his compliance with the request and for the interest he has taken in the progress of the work.

EDGAR PRESTAGE.

Chapters in
Anglo-Portuguese Relations

Chapter I.

The English Crusaders in Portugal.

When the Arabs conquered Spain in the early part of the eighth century, they occupied also the whole of the later kingdom of Portugal, and held it for more than three centuries. They and their Berber allies settled in large numbers throughout the country, increased and multiplied, and in spite of stormy episodes in their history, developed agriculture and commerce to a high pitch. But we must not forget that though the Arab and Berber elements in the population were certainly large, during those three centuries a considerable number of the original inhabitants of the country also embraced the religion of Islam and intermarried with them. When we speak of the Moors in Spain and Portugal, we are speaking of a mixed population, Muslims by religion, but who used the Galician Romance language alongside of, and perhaps even more than Arabic. Consequently, there was no great gulf of race or language between them and their Christian fellow-countrymen, the Mozarabs, who, though holding to their old religion, participated fully in the social and economic life of the cities and the countryside, and to a considerable extent in their cultural life as well.

A

This cultural life centred mainly on the cities, some of which, such as Lisbon and Evora, were older than the Arab conquest, others, like Alcacer and Silves, new creations. We are accustomed to look upon the Portuguese provinces as rather neglected outposts of the Arab empire, but the error of this view is shown by the large number of Moorish cities which they contained, and the many traces of their occupation which are still to be found throughout the length and breadth of the country. Most of the cities were, of course, fortified, and contained an inner castle occupied by the troops of the governor. The early fortifications were not, apparently, very substantial, and were probably intended chiefly to provide a refuge against the attacks of the Norsemen and the Christians of the North. So long as the western part of the Peninsula formed outlying provinces of a central power, there was little object in building strong castles which might be assaulted and captured before the troops of the central authority could intervene, and thus become centres of resistance to reconquest. There are, in fact, several instances of the temporary capture or occupation of these outlying cities in the ninth, tenth and eleventh centuries; Lisbon, for example, was sacked by the Christian kings of Galicia in 798 and again about 950.[1]

The strengthening of the fortifications must accordingly be put not earlier than the middle or so of the eleventh century. The history of other Muslim countries, including North-West Africa, suggests that the work of fortification was most active during periods of disintegration, when a number of rival petty kingdoms were set up. Each prince naturally

[1]The occupation of Santarem and Lisbon by Alfonso VI of Leon in 1093 was not by conquest, but by temporary cession; see Dozy, *Histoire des Musulmans d'Espagne*, III, 152.

2

fortified his capital as strongly as possible against the attacks of his rivals, and at the same time built a number of forts in other places to serve as *points d'appui* against hostile incursions and as bases for his own raids into hostile territories. This corresponds pretty well to the situation in the Peninsula during a large part of the eleventh and first half of the twelfth centuries.

Such a unity as had been built up round the Caliphate of Cordova in the tenth century was succeeded in the eleventh by the disintegration of Peninsular Islam into a score of petty " kingdoms," most of which were subsequently brought under the precarious suzerainty of Seville. Towards the close of the century, the Muslim provinces were annexed to the empire of the Berber Almoravids of Morocco, but it is doubtful how far their writ ran in the more distant regions. The decline of the Almoravid empire and their evacuation of Andalusia in 1138 produced a fresh outcrop of petty principalities, and provided an opportunity of which Alfonso of Aragon, on the one hand, and the rulers of the new principality of Portugal on the other, took advantage to extend their respective territories.

It is scarcely necessary at this point to relate the troubled beginnings of the new state—how an ambitious Burgundian knight, Henrique, who had come to seek his fortune in the Peninsula under the banner of Leon, was given the honourable but dangerous frontier provinces of Braga and Coimbra in fief at the close of the eleventh century, with the title of Count of Portucal ; and how, after his death in 1114, his widow, Theresa, the illegitimate daughter of Alfonso of Leon, maintained his country against her relatives, until her young son Alfonso assumed control and demonstrated his independence, first by exiling his mother and then by open warfare with the forces

3

of Leon. These activities had precluded for the time being any serious attempt to extend the frontiers of the county southwards at the expense of the Moors. But when, about 1137, a sort of equilibrium was established between the Christian states of the Peninsula, Alfonso at once turned his attention in that direction, with the double object of making his independence more secure and of increasing the economic strength of his principality.

The Portuguese historians generally confess themselves at a loss to understand the political situation amongst the Moors in their country at this time, and the Arabic chroniclers certainly leave many points open to question. But their narratives can fortunately be supplemented from the descriptions of the famous Arabic geographer Idrīsī, who had himself visited Lisbon just before the Portuguese conquest.[1] Idrīsī distinguishes three provinces in this part of the Peninsula : (1) al-Qunu,[2] including Santa-Maria (Faro), Mértola and Silves ; (2) al-Qasr, including Alcacer, Evora, Badajoz, Xeres (de los Cavalleros), Mérida, Alcantara and Coria ; (3) Balāta, including Santarem, Lisbon and Sintra.

Are these provinces delimited geographically or politically ? It seems probable that the division is at least qualified by political considerations,[3] since geographically there is little connection between Mértola and Silves or between Badajoz and Alcacer. On the decay of the Almoravid power, we find the southern part of Portugal subject to two princes, both

---

[1]Edrîsî, text, pp. 184, 7.

[2]In the printed text "al-Faghar," but Professor David Lopes has shown that the name is probably arabicized from the old Roman name Cuneus (*Boletim* III, 212-213).

[3]Professor Lopes, however, suggests that it is derived from the division found in the work of the Latin geographer, Pomponius Mela (*ibid.*, 214-216).

of local and non-Arab origin, one of whom, Ibn Qasī, held Mértola, with a subordinate governor in Silves, and the other, Sīdrāy[1] ibn Wazīr, held Evora and Badajoz. The two princes, as usual, were bitter rivals but the general situation remained unchanged, Ibn Qasī allying himself with the new and rising power of the Almohads in Morocco, and Sīdrāy, as we learn from the English chronicler Osbern, with Alfonso Henriques of Portugal. The position in Balāta is more obscure. From Christian sources we learn that the cities paid tribute to Alfonso Henriques, but they certainly did not form part of the dominions of Sīdrāy. The most probable solution is that they were constituted as independent republics, and Osbern gives us a glimpse of a senate at Lisbon composed of the military commander, the Christian bishop, and the chief citizens.[2]

Idrīsī, however, gives also detailed descriptions of the cities, which are interesting enough to occupy us for a few moments. In the southern province (Algarve), Silves was evidently the capital town. Idrīsī describes it as a pleasant city, situated in a plain and surrounded by a strong wall, with a port on the river which flows on its southern side, and a shipyard. " It is of fine appearance, with attractive buildings and well-furnished bazaars. Its inhabitants . . . are Yemenite Arabs and others,[3] who speak the pure Arabic language, compose poetry, and are eloquent in

[1]So according to the spelling of Ibn Sahib as-Salah (ap. Lopes, *Boletim*, III 373, 9). From the unique dirham preserved in the British Museum (Vol. V p. 82, No. 230), it is clear that he acknowledged at first the suzerainty of the Amir of Cordova, Hamdin.

[2]Osbernus, ed. Stubbs, clxi.

[3]The non-Arab element was probably more prominent than this phrase would suggest, since Ibn al-Mundhir, who assumed control of Silves after the assassination of Ibn Qasi in 1151, was a *muwallad* or " new Muslim " of an influential family in the city (*Boletim* III, 334).

5

speech and elegant in manners, both upper and lower classes." He describes also the great church of St. Vincent on the Cape—no one, he says, may pass that way without partaking of its hospitality. "This is an immutable obligation and perpetual custom, from which they never depart, inherited from generation to generation . . . This church . . . possesses vast treasures and ample revenues, mainly derived from lands with which it has been endowed in different parts of Algarve." This description is worth bearing in mind in connection with what will be said later on the relations of the Christian Mozarabs to their Muslim overlords and the foreign Crusaders.

In the province of Alemtejo, Idrīsī describes Alcacer as a pleasant town of medium size and with important shipyards. Evora was, however, the principal city, "large and populous, with a wall, castle and cathedral mosque." Of Lisbon he says only that it is "a fine city, extending along the Tagus, with a wall and a strong castle, and containing springs which are warm in winter and in summer,"[1] and then breaks off to tell a long story of eight "adventurers" of Lisbon who set out on an expedition over the "Sea of Darkness" (the Ocean) "to find out what it contained and how far it extended," an interesting indication that already in the Muslim period, Portuguese seamen were boldly setting out on quests of exploration.[2] He next mentions Santarem, describing it as an unwalled city on a high hill. The Christian chronicler, Galvão, also describes it as unwalled, except for the fort,[3] which is

[1]Hence the name *Alfama* (Arabic *al-hamma*, " warm spring ") still borne by the quarter of the present city which occupies the eastern half of the site of the old Moorish city.

[2]Edrīsī, pp. 184-185. The story is quoted in full by Beazley, *The Dawn of Modern Geography*, III, 532.

[3]A. Botelho da Costa Veiga : *Duarte Galvão e sua Cronica*, (Lisbon, 1932), p. 12.

significant as showing that Santarem, though of strategic value, was not regarded as an important city at that time. Of Sintra, Idrīsī says nothing at all.

*   *   *

Alfonso Henriques began his campaigns by building or rebuilding fortresses at Leiria and other points on his southern frontiers, and by raiding the Muslim territories. He met with but indifferent success at first, and it was not until March, 1147, that the first important conquest was made, when Santarem was captured in a bold night assault led by the king himself. But the little kingdom was too small and poor to venture on any large enterprise against the stronger Muslim states. For this task, it was necessary to find allies and one can well understand that Alfonso was unwilling to give any pretext for intervention to the more powerful and jealous Christian states of Spain. But, precisely at this juncture, the forces of which he was in such need came within reach of his hand, and with rare tact and skill he seized the opportunity.

We need not recapitulate here the history of that species of *Völkerwanderung* which we call the Crusades, but may refer only to one aspect of them which is sometimes overlooked. When we number the more important episodes successively as First Crusade, Second Crusade, Third Crusade and so on, we ought not to forget that the Crusades were in reality sustained by a constant succession of small bands of pilgrims coming from all parts of Europe to strike a blow for the Faith. Most of these, from France, Southern Germany and the Mediterranean countries, took the land route or sailed from the Italian ports, but those from the maritime north-western countries of Europe, on the other hand, preferred the long sea route through the Strait of Gibraltar.

7

The reason for this preference was not entirely their greater familiarity with the sea, but rather that for these maritime peoples, very different from the Franks and the Italians in manners and culture, the voyage to Jerusalem was only an extension of long-established relations with the western coasts of the Peninsula. These relations go back to the ninth and tenth centuries, when bands of Norsemen sacked and pillaged not only the coast towns, but also inland towns like Beja, and even Seville and Cordova (in 844). It was probably to resist their raids that the first fortifications were constructed. Various Christianized elements also joined with the Norse in these piratical raids, chiefly from England and Brittany, but there is little evidence that any distinction was made between the treatment of Christian and Muslim territories, even after the Norsemen themselves were converted. The exploits, for instance, of Olaf Haraldsson (known to later generations as St. Olave), not only in Kent, Touraine and Poitou, but also in Galicia in 1013-1014, show how slightly religious considerations weighed with the invaders.

Even Sigurd the Jorsalafar, on his famous pilgrimage, seized the castle and possessions of the Christian count of Galicia, before sailing down the Iberian coast in 1108 and raiding the Muslim towns of Sintra, Lisbon and Alcacer on the way. Three years later, during the civil war in Leon, two Galician nobles (to quote the Chronicle of Compostella) " hired the assistance of certain pirates who had arrived in Spain from England for the purpose of proceeding to Jerusalem . . . which English, suddenly invading the maritime regions from the sea, murdered some and robbed others of all they possessed, and, as though they were Moors, seized and fettered others for ransom, violated the churches and sacrilegiously carried off whatsoever

8

necessaries were found in them and even men," until
" by the intercession of St. James " and other more
forcible measures the bishop of Compostella succeeded
in driving them off to pursue their attacks upon the
Muslim foe. By the middle of the twelfth century,
indeed, the English were so familiar on the coasts of
Spain that Idrīsī calls the Bay of Biscay the " Sea of
the English."[1]

Alfonso Henriques was thus following an established,
if dangerous, practice, but with the merit of employing
the foreign Crusaders against Muslim enemies, not
against Christian rivals. And the moment itself, as
we have seen, was propitious, when the breakdown of
the Almoravid empire and the mutual jealousy of the
Muslim princes rendered it less likely that effective
support would be forthcoming for the attacked.

The first experiment, however, was unsuccessful.
Sometime about 1140 a fleet of sixty or seventy ships
proceeding to the Holy Land, together with some
Anglo-Normans and others, was persuaded to assist
in an attack on Lisbon. The besiegers were apparently
let down by some slackness on the part of the Portuguese
levies, and the memory of this failure nearly com-
promised the next attack at its very outset. For the
fleet that came in 1147 included a squadron led by
two Anglo-Norman pirates, named William and
Radulf, with men of Bristol and Hampshire, who had
taken part also in the earlier expedition.

This fleet consisted of some 190 vessels, the nucleus
being formed by Rhinelanders and Flemings, who had
responded to the call of St. Bernard of Clairvaux, then
engaged in preaching the Second Crusade to recover
Edessa from the infidel. At Dartmouth, they were
joined by a roughly equal number of Anglo-Normans,
commanded by four constables, together with some

[1]Edrîsî, p. 173, 16-17 : *bahr al-Anqalishin.*

9

Scots and Bretons, and the combined fleet set sail with about 10,000 Crusaders on board on 23rd May, 1147, and reached Oporto on 16th June. The story of the events that followed was told by several of those who took part in them, but in the fullest and most accurate detail by an English Crusader named Osbern. His narrative is recognised to be without question the most authentic source for the history[1] of the capture of Lisbon, and has the further interest for us of being the first known work dealing with the Crusades by an English writer.

At Oporto the bishop of the town, on behalf of the King of Portugal, welcomed the pilgrims with a long sermon, at the end of which he engaged them by handsome promises to assist the king in the capture of Lisbon. They accepted the offer, and on 28th June, anchored in the Tagus. Osbern describes the city in glowing terms : " most opulent with the products of all Africa and a great part of Europe, its surrounding territory second to none in fertility . . . the summit of the hill girt with a circular wall, the city-walls descending the slope to right and to left down to the bank of the Tagus, with dependent suburbs below the wall hewn out in the rock in rows, so that each row might be regarded as a castle of the utmost strength, for with so many obstacles is it surrounded—populous beyond reckoning, for, as we learned from their Alcaide, that is governor, after the capture of the city, this city had 154,000 men exclusive of women and children, but reckoning in the citizens expelled in this year from the Castle of Santarem . . . and all the leading citizens of Sintra, Almada and Palmella, from all parts of Spain and Africa, and many merchants. But in spite of their being so many, they possessed an armoury of lances and shields sufficient for only 15,000 men, and with these they made sorties in turns."

On the following day, 29th June, Alfonso Henriques arrived with his forces, and was nearly overwhelmed by the mob of excited pilgrims. But his request that they should choose leaders to debate with him the terms upon which they would give their assistance threatened to wreck the undertaking at the very outset. The German-Flemish contingent agreed without delay, but in the English camp there was some dissension. Our two pirates, William and Radulf, with their followers from Southampton and Hastings, argued that the king's word was not to be trusted—much better continue the journey along the Spanish coast, plundering the ships and merchants on the way, and not lose the favourable weather for the voyage to Jerusalem. But the constable of Suffolk, Hervey of Glanvill, delivered a moving speech, upbraiding them for their disloyalty to their comrades. " Take example from your neighbours ; the men of Cologne do not dispute with the men of Cologne, the Flemings do not show jealousy of the Flemings. Who would deny that the Scots are barbarians ?—but even they have never failed in the duty of friendship between us." Thus, supported by the majority of the English, he gained the consent of William to remain—so long as supplies were regularly maintained and not a day longer.

The terms were then drawn up with the King of Portugal. On the capture of Lisbon, all the possessions of the enemy should belong exclusively to the Crusaders together with all sums of money paid for ransoms ; they should occupy the city until it was completely sacked ; the city and rural properties should be divided amongst those who chose to remain in Portugal, each enjoying the liberties of his own country, under the dominion of the Portuguese crown ; and all participants, together with their heirs and successors, should be exempt from tolls, dues and customs for their ships and merchandise in all parts of Portugal. The King further swore not to quit the camp, unless on extreme necessity or if the enemy invaded his territories.

The authorities of the city, including the Mozarab bishop, having rejected the usual formal invitation to surrender, the siege was formed—Alfonso on the north side, the Anglo-Norman contingent on the west, the Germans and Dutch on the east. On June 30th, a general assault was repulsed, but some Anglo-Normans succeeded in forcing an entry into the south-western suburb, and maintained their position through the night and against a counter-attack the following morning. This success, almost on the first day, greatly contributed to the ultimate conquest of the city, since the captured suburb contained the matamores or grainstores of the city, in which, says Osbern, there were found a hundred thousand loads of cereals and vegetables. The siege was to last for nearly four months more, but the assaults of the besiegers were now seconded by increasing famine within the city. The actual details of the siege may be passed over; there were the usual attempts to construct siege machinery and to undermine the walls, with little success on the whole. In August, as the Crusaders were beginning to flag, some correspondence between the citizens and the governor of Evora was intercepted. The citizens had appealed to Evora for assistance, exposing their dangerous situation, but the governor (presumably Sīdrāy ibn Wazīr) replied coldly that as an ally of the Portuguese he could not intervene. It has been plausibly suggested that the correspondence was a stratagem on the part of Alfonso Henriques, but whatever truth there may be in that, it is certain that no help came, and that the Crusaders were spurred on to further efforts.

While the Anglo-Normans prepared new siege engines, the Germans and Flemings succeeded in undermining a part of the city wall and made a breach of thirty cubits. Nevertheless, the garrison hastily set up a rampart and repulsed all attempts to penetrate into the city. This produced a curious incident, which illustrates the jealousy existing between the two contingents of the Crusading army. The Anglo-Normans, eager to second the efforts of the Germans, hurried round to the eastern side, " but were assailed with abuse by the leaders of the Flemish and Rhine-landers, who demanded that we should try to make our own entrance in whatever way we could with the help of our machines, for this entrance which was now opened up belonged to them and not to us." There are many passages in Osbern's narrative which betray the same jealousy and dislike of the Germans and Flemish on the part of the Anglo-Normans.

The breach in the east wall had been made on 16th October. On the 20th, the Anglo-Normans, with the Portuguese, began to move their great new tower up to the south-western angle of the wall. The garrison, though reduced to the utmost extremity of famine, fought with the courage of despair. When the high tides surrounded the tower during the evening and again in the early morning, they tried to destroy it by means of incendiary projectiles, combined with sorties. But the attack was successfully repulsed, seven men of Ipswich particularly distinguishing themselves in the defence. At ten o'clock on the morning of the 21st, the tower was moved closer to the wall and the scaling bridge thrown out. Then at last the Moors capitulated and asked for terms, giving in the meantime five hostages to Hervey of Glanvill, who handed them over to the king. This act nearly caused a mutiny among the Crusaders, who, now that victory was within their grasp, imagined that they were about to be cheated of the prizes promised to them by the king, "for such was his custom," adds Osbern. The English sailors, stirred up by a Bristol priest—" a man of the worst morals (asserts Osbern), as we found out later on when he was caught redhanded in robberies "—rushed to the king's camp, shouting " Down with the traitor " and demanding that Hervey should be handed over to them for punishment. The tumult was pacified by some of the English leaders, and negotiations were resumed. But the Moors now intervened, declaring that they were ready to carry out their promises and more to the king, but with the Crusaders they would have nothing to do but fight to the death, for they were " an immoral, faithless, disloyal and ferocious folk, who would not spare even their own chiefs." The conditions finally agreed to by Alfonso were that the governor and his son-in-law alone should retain their belongings, and that all the other citizens should vacate the city with nothing but the victuals they possessed. This provoked a fresh outburst among the Crusaders, for which Osbern blames (probably unjustly) the Rhinelanders and Flemings, " born greedy." The German commander in particular insisted that he must have the governor's Arab mare. The king, in disgust, declared that rather than yield to such a disloyal rabble he would withdraw from the siege, for honour was dearer to him than even the possession of Lisbon. By next morning, however, tempers had calmed, and the Crusaders accepted the conditions and swore homage to the king.

It was arranged that 300 men, 160 Germans and Flemings and 140 Anglo-Normans, should occupy the city to see to the execution of the terms. On the 24th the gates were opened and the 300 men, followed by the king with his Portuguese knights, marched up

14

to the castle, planted the cross, and sang a *Te Deum*. Meanwhile the other Crusaders had rushed into the city and begun to plunder and ill-use the inhabitants ; the Mozarab bishop was killed, and the Count of Aerschot forcibly seized the coveted mare. Osbern blames, as usual, the Rhinelanders and Flemings— " the Normans and English, however, most steadfast to their word and religion, considering what such an action might portend, remained quietly in their appointed place, preferring to withhold their hands from all rapine than to violate their oath of fidelity and comradeship." In view of what had gone before and was to come, as we shall see, it is a little hard to believe in Osbern's protestations. At length, however, order was restored and for three days the exodus of the population continued, leaving behind them such heaps of dead and dying as shocked even the Crusaders.

So ended the siege of Lisbon, in striking contrast to the miserable history of the Second Crusade in Syria, a contrast which is suitably and edifyingly stressed by all the English chroniclers of the time. " Truly," says Henry of Huntingdon,[1] " God opposes the proud, but shows grace to the humble. For the army of the king of France and the emperor of Germany was more splendid and numerous than that which first made the conquest of Jerusalem, and was ground to powder by some few men, and swept away like spiders' webs ; whereas to these men of low degree no multitude could oppose resistance." But we cannot help sharing the sentiments of the Portuguese historians who, in the midst of their jubilation over the conquest, yet pause to admire the heroism of the citizens who put up so magnificent a defence in the face of famine and every discouragement.

This obstinate resistance is particularly noteworthy

[1]Ed. T. Arnold (Rolls Series, London, 1879), p. 281.

15

when we reflect that a large proportion of the citizens, possibly as much as the half,[1] were not Muslims but Mozarabs. Whatever the attitude of these may have been towards the Portuguese, it is clear that they were fully as determined in their opposition to the Crusaders as were the Muslims, and were ready to share the fortunes of the latter to the end. To the northern Crusaders, whose prime object was booty, wherever or however got, there was no distinction between them.[2] But it was not Alfonso's policy to lose such valuable subjects and see wide areas of his country laid desolate. While large grants of land were made, in fulfilment of his promises, to those of the Crusaders who elected to remain behind in Portugal when the remainder continued their journey to the East, we shall see that he very soon took his former enemies under his protection and granted them full rights of residence and property in their former cities.

Meanwhile, he prepared to extend his conquests across the Tagus. Sintra and Palmella, their defenders having disappeared with the fall of Lisbon, had surrendered without a blow, and Palmella in particular, garrisoned by the military orders (and perhaps reconstructed), served as a valuable advanced base for raids into Alemtejo. The next place of importance was Alcacer do Sal (Al-Qasr ibn Abī Dānis), then little inferior to Lisbon as a port, and garrisoned, according to the Gothic Chronicle, by 500 horsemen and 10,000 infantry. After the capture of Lisbon, Alfonso had appointed an English priest, Gilbert, as first bishop of the new see, and he now sent this man, about 1151, to

[1] *Cf.* the statement in *Heimskringla* (trans. Laing[2] [London, 1889], Vol. IV p. 119): " Lisbon, a great city in Spain, half Christian and half heathen."

[2] Even the cleric Osbern, though he knows of the bishop and presumably therefore of the existence of other Christians in the city, shares to a large extent the common misunderstanding.

16

England to preach a crusade against the "Moors of Seville," in preparation for an attack on Alcacer. An English fleet duly arrived and took part in a general assault on the town, but failed to capture it. It is curious to recall that in the winter of 1152, probably the same year as this attack, occurred the last Norse incursion on the Peninsular coast, when Ronald, earl of Orkney, destroyed a castle in Galicia on his way to Jerusalem.

For a long time after this, there is no further word of English Crusaders in Portugal. Alcacer was again unsuccessfully attacked in 1157 with the aid of Flemish Crusaders, but was captured by the Portuguese unaided in the following year. During the next decade, in spite of occasional setbacks, Alfonso's authority was gradually extended over the cities and fortresses of Alemtejo, mainly through the exploits of Gerald the Fearless. In 1170, Alfonso, who had now, on account of advancing years, associated his son Sancho with him in the kingdom, found the situation sufficiently stable to issue a charter " to you Moors who are enfranchised (*forri*) in Lisbon, Almada, Palmella and Alcacer," granting them immunity from injury and laying down legislation concerning them.[1] That this was no mere formality, we shall see shortly.

The success of the Portuguese king in Alemtejo was, no doubt, due largely to the pre-occupation of the Muslim rulers of Andalusia, the Almohads of Morocco, with other problems. Nevertheless, they kept a watchful eye upon these distant frontiers, and when in 1178, Sancho led a raid upon Triana, the southern suburb of Seville, the cup was full. A raid by land upon Evora and by sea upon Lisbon in 1179 preceded a general invasion conducted by the Almohad Caliph (Abū Yaʻqūb Yūsuf) in person in 1184. The main

[1]*Port. Mon. hist., Chartæ*, Vol. I, pp. 396-397.

assault was delivered upon Santarem, but when the city was on the point of capture, the Caliph suddenly fell ill and the siege was abandoned. He died during the retreat to Seville, and internal disorders prevented a renewal of the attack for some years.

Sancho, his dominions in Alemtejo thus restored to him, now began to cast envious eyes on the rich lands of Algarve. It will be remembered that in 1187 Saladin had recovered Jerusalem, and in the following year the countries of Northern and Western Europe began to make preparations for the Third Crusade. Simultaneously, Sancho prepared to follow his father's example in making use of such fleets as might enter Portuguese waters. The first to arrive was a Danish and Frisian fleet of some 50 or 60 vessels, in the spring of 1189. These were joined by a Portuguese fleet, and on their route southwards they turned aside to the minor fortress of Alvōr, on the eastern side of the Bay of Lagos, and having sacked it, continued their journey to Palestine.

In July, 36 ships reached Lisbon from Germany and Holland with 3,500 Crusaders on board, a large number being Englishmen, chiefly from London, who had been picked up at Dartmouth. The Portuguese fleet now joined this squadron, and they sailed for Silves. The siege of the city was formed on 21st July, and Sancho arrived with his land forces on the 29th. The first assaults were unsuccessful, but early in August the Crusaders captured an outwork on the river and thus cut off the town from its water supply. Although there was a large cistern, still in good condition to-day, in the interior of the castle, the amount of water it contained was insufficient to supply the needs of the city, and thirst now began to second the efforts of the besiegers. But a general assault on 18th August was beaten off so decisively that the Portuguese talked of raising the siege. The Crusaders, however, eager for the spoils of the city, insisted on remaining and began to dig a mine. The garrison countermined and a fierce battle was joined in the bowels of the earth. Again the Crusaders were forced to retire. Soon afterwards, however, the terrible ravages of thirst forced the garrison to ask for terms and beg to be allowed to evacuate the city with their movable goods. Sancho agreed, but the Crusaders vigorously protested. In vain the king offered to buy the town from them for 10,000 pieces of gold[1]—for 20,000 pieces of gold ; nothing would satisfy them but unconditional surrender. On 3rd September, the gates were opened, and the population, reduced to 16,000 souls, began to file out, to be bullied and stripped of their clothing by the Crusaders, as they made their way towards Seville. On the following night Sancho occupied the castle with his Portuguese, and the Crusaders began to sack the city. But not for long ; for a dispute having suddenly arisen over the distribution of the grainstores, Sancho sent out his troops, drove the Crusaders from the city, and refused to re-admit them. After waiting for twelve days, to share out the spoils they had acquired, they went on their way, some to Syria, some back to their own countries, but most of them loudly accusing the Portuguese of having taken no part either in the siege works or in the fighting and done nothing all the time but insult the " Christians," and then in the end having defrauded them of their due.[2]

Of all their possessions in Portugal, nothing was now left to the Moors but Faro, Tavira, Mértola, and perhaps Beja. Nevertheless, Sancho had in reality

[1]It is noteworthy that these are specifically called *morabitini*, i.e. Almoravid dinars.

[2]" Princeps civitatis vocatus *Alcad* regem adiit *Portugalensem*, qui cum exercitu supervenerat sed Christianis nullum præstabat auxilium " (Radulf of Diceto).

taken on more than he could maintain. The Portuguese forces were still too weak to hold the great tracts of land in the south, most of which were in fact garrisoned by the Knights Templars and other military orders. Their feudal levies were exhausted by the continual warfare of many decades, not only against the Moors, but also against Leon. At this juncture the Almohads again counter-attacked, and it is in this connection that we hear for the last time of English Crusaders in Portugal, in an episode which exemplifies both their good qualities at their best and their indiscipline at its worst.

In 1190 the new Almohad Caliph, Abū Yūsuf Ya'qūb, resolved to avenge his father's failure and death at Santarem. Ordering the governor of Cordova to assemble the Andalusian levies, he crossed the Straits with his Moroccan troops in the spring, and the joint forces marched on Silves. Leaving the Andalusians there, he himself with his Africans turned northwards and at the end of June crossed the Tagus and invaded Estremadura. Sancho found himself in a difficult situation; his troops were few, and in face of the Almohad raids could not be safely concentrated in one place. Most opportunely, a fresh English fleet was just setting out to join Richard in Palestine. During a storm in the Bay of Biscay, the first squadron of ten ships was dispersed. A few days later, one solitary ship crept hesitatingly with a hundred Crusaders on board, not knowing where they were, into the Bay of Silves. The new Flemish bishop begged for their aid in repelling the expected attack on the city, and the gallant hundred not only joined the garrison, but also broke up their ship for defensive works on a guarantee that they would be indemnified—a guarantee which was duly observed later on.

Meanwhile Sancho, rightly convinced that the

Caliph would sooner or later attack Santarem, had thrown himself with his personal troops into the city. Suddenly the nine other ships appeared in the Tagus. On an urgent appeal from Sancho, a force of five hundred men, " well-armed, and the pick of all those who had come in the vessels, the braver and more spirited of them, preferring rather to die in warfare for the name of Jesus Christ than to see the misfortunes and extermination of their own people," marched up to Santarem, and provided a welcome reinforcement for the small garrison. At the end of June, the Moroccan troops prepared to lay siege to Santarem, after Sancho had rejected a proposal for a seven years' truce on condition of the surrender of Silves. Only a day or two later, however, the Caliph's army was seen to be in full retreat, probably, as the Portuguese historians have conjectured, on account of the losses caused by the fevers which infest the Tagus valley in summer. The English chronicler, on the other hand, has no doubts that the retreat was due to the fear inspired in the Caliph by the intervention of the English Crusaders.[1]

It would be pleasant to end the story here, with Sancho's protestations of undying gratitude to his gallant helpers. Unfortunately, it has a sequel. Scarcely had the Moroccan forces withdrawn than the 63 remaining ships of the English fleet arrived at Lisbon. The Crusaders landed, and, incredible as it may seem (though it is an English chronicler who tells the story), began to rob, burn and plunder in the city and its environs, and to do violence to the citizens, particularly at the expense of the Moors and Jews who were living there under Portuguese protection. Sancho hastened down from Santarem and, still grateful for

[1]Kurth, however (p. 211), is of opinion that the retreat was really caused by the arrival of the main English fleet.

the aid received from their comrades, took the moderate course of persuading the commanders to recall their men and make them swear to observe the police regulations of Richard Cœur-de-Lion, whose drastic provisions show that he at least had no illusions about the character of his subjects. But only three days later, a dispute broke out, leading to fresh affrays with the citizens and renewed violence. Sancho this time lost patience; he had the gates closed, ordered out the Portuguese garrison in the citadel, and took all the English in the city into custody, to the number of 700. Before releasing them, he demanded the restitution of stolen goods and arms and an undertaking to respect the peace in all ports of his kingdom. So, on 24th July, the fleet sailed on its way, leaving behind it a very mixed memory of the English Crusaders in Portugal.

The sole permanent result of their several interventions was, after all, the conquest of Lisbon.[1] In the very next year, 1191, the Almohads reappeared and this time recovered not only Silves and Algarve, but also the whole of Alemtejo, with the exception of Evora, and it was not until 1250 that these provinces were finally incorporated into the kingdom of Portugal. But the capture of Lisbon was probably the decisive event in the creation of the kingdom, and we do well to recall occasionally the share of our countrymen in this half-forgotten exploit, the most successful and least questionable of all the Crusades.

[1]Among the Crusaders who remained in Portugal after the conquest, and who were granted lands and immunities, were certainly a number of Anglo-Normans, as is shown by the names preserved in various Portuguese documents. Since the Crusaders laid such stress upon freedom of trade in the terms agreed to with Alfonso, it is very probable that one result was to open up commercial relations between Portugal and England, as well as the other northern countries (*cf.* Kurth, 246 ff.).

Bibliography.

A. Herculano : *Historia de Portugal,* 8° ed., dirigida por David Lopes.

Historia de Portugal, edicão monumental commemorativa do 8° Centenario da fundação da nacionalidade, Vol. II (Barcelos, 1929).

Idrîsî : *Description de l'Afrique et de l'Espagne par Edrîsî,* publiée avec une traduction par R. Dozy et M. J. de Goeje (Leide, 1866).

Osbernus de Expugnatione Lyxbonensi, ed. W. Stubbs in *Chronicles and Memorials of the Reign of Richard I,* Vol. I (Rolls Series, London, 1864), pp. cxlii-clxxxii, [also under title "Crucesignati Anglici Epistola," together with the Epistle of Arnulf, in *Portugaliæ Mon. Hist., Scriptores,* Vol. I, 392-407].

Radulf of Diceto : *Ymagines Historiarum,* in *Historiæ Anglicanæ Scriptores X* (London, 1652), coll. 645-646.

Roger of Hoveden : *Chronica,* ed. W. Stubbs (Rolls Series), Vol. III, pp. 42-45.

R. Dozy : *Recherches sur l'histoire et la littérature de l'Espagne pendant le moyen âge,* 3me ed., T. II (Paris-Leide, 1881).

David Lopes : "Os arabes nas obras de Alexandre Herculano,' in *Academia das Sciencias de Lisboa, Boletim da Segunda Classe* Vol. III (1909-1910) and Vol. IV (1910-1911).

Friedrich Kurth : "Der Anteil niederdeutscher Kreuzfahrer an den Kämpfen der Portugesien gegen den Mauren," in *Mitteilungen für österreichische Geschichtsforschung,* VIII. Ergänzungsband, 1. Heft (Innsbruck, 1909).

L. Saavedra Machado : "Os Ingleses em Portugal," in *Biblos,* (Coimbra : Revista da Faculdade de Letras), Vol. IX (1933).

CHAPTER II.

The Expedition of John of Gaunt to the Peninsular.

On March 25th, 1386, John of Gaunt, fourth son of Edward III, was preparing to leave England for a castle in Spain. According to a contemporary historian he and his wife took part in a pleasing court ceremony before they left. Their nephew, Richard II, wished them god-speed, thoughtfully provided them with two golden crowns, and expressed the wish that his subjects should call them the king and queen of Spain and should give them the royal honours due to their rank. English historians, intent on the domestic problems of the period, usually have no time to do more than hint as they pass, that Richard had considerable satisfaction in speeding the parting guests. John of Gaunt, by the grace of God, King of Castile, Leon, Toledo, Galicia, Seville, Cordova, Murcia, Jaen, Algarve and Algeciras, Duke of Aquitaine and Lancaster, Earl of Derby, Lincoln, Leicester and Lord of Molina—to give him the accumulation of titles he had been using for some years—was a disturbing element amongst the English nobility, and an uncomfortable presence near his nephew's throne. There was much to be said for encouraging an expedition to a country where he and his consort might wear those golden crowns.

It is not for us to follow out the implications of that

cynical suggestion. What we have to attempt is a
different task. We have picked up a fragment in the
mosaic of Anglo-Portuguese relations. By itself it
means little or nothing. Can we put it back into the
pattern where it belongs, so that it will take on a
meaning ? Can this adventure be made to look a little
less madcap, a little more logical ? We can try, but if
we are to succeed we must be prepared to handle the
other pieces of the mosaic so as to fit the fourteenth
century adventure connected with the name of John of
Gaunt into its proper setting in the story of Anglo-
Portuguese relationships. There are, of course, ways
of evading such responsibility. One of them is to
dismiss the whole affair, as the chronicler Knighton
did, without too much introspection. " And so," he
says in his account of the Duke's expedition, " he
directed his steps towards the port of Plymouth to set
out with his army for Spain, in accordance with the
will of God." But to some of us will occur the fancy
that the chronicler had failed to detect the busy fingers
of quite a few men who were playing with those pieces.
They will have to be noticed if we would remake the
mosaic. In such a task, two very general rules may
guide us by indicating the nature of the pattern that
ought to come through.

The first of these generalisations concerns the space
the adventure occupies in time. To appreciate its
significance it will be necessary to deal with the section
of Anglo-Portuguese relations that falls within the limits
of the years 1349 and 1387. The first of these dates is
an arbitrary choice but there is some justification for it,
since it was the year when John of Gaunt was old
enough—he was ten—to be present at his first battle.
The affair was a fitting prelude to his career, for it was
a sea-fight, and the enemy ships involved were ships
belonging to Castile. There is another reason for

choosing it. The year 1349 is something of a landmark in Castilian history, for it marks the death of Alfonso XI, the king of that country. There need be no hesitation in the selection of the closing date. Indeed, it forces itself upon us, since it is the year when John of Gaunt's treaty with the King of Castile was concluded, and the episode in Anglo-Portuguese relations with which his name is so closely connected was declared closed.

The second guide to our problem is a simplification which provides a clue to what is a very complex series of diplomatic relations. The essentials are three, and it is the interactions between them that make history. The three are Castile, John of Gaunt and Portugal. The task before anyone trying to understand John of Gaunt's expedition to the Peninsula is to see through the eyes of the Englishman what was taking place in Castile and Portugal, so as to understand his reaction to those events.

That word "events" suggests that there are some to whom they are valueless, unless they are dated and arranged chronologically. For them a scheme may be suggested which clarifies, without being more misleading than such arbitrary classifications inevitably must be. Roughly, the events of the period 1349—1387 may be grouped into three phases. From 1349—1367 the events most worthy of attention are concerned, in the main, with Castile. From 1367—1371 interest shifts to John of Gaunt. From 1371—1387 the outstanding factor is Portugal. But since this third phase is the climax of the story, it is naturally more complicated, for in those last years all the elements come into prominence and events significant for each of the three have to be kept in mind. With some reservations, such an arrangement of the facts will serve as a framework. It suggests that our problem can be reduced to its lowest terms. The first phase gave, in Castile, the motive for the expedition ; the second, in John of Gaunt, gave the man ; the third, in Portugal, gave the opportunity.

Although primarily of importance for Castilian history, the first phase (1349-1367) was also charged with meaning for Anglo-Portuguese relations. First and foremost the events of those years reveal Castile as a storm centre. Without the questions raised in that part of the Peninsula, John of Gaunt might never have embarked upon his enterprise, and a large part of his life work would not have been. Further, this first phase illustrates very clearly the special curse of Spanish politics in the later Middle Ages. The sooner we appreciate the part played by internal feuds and dynastic quarrels in disturbing the relations between Castile and Portugal and in reducing the former to impotence, the sooner we shall see how and why a foreigner like John of Gaunt managed to come into the story. There is another reason why this phase is important. It shows how the affairs of these two states were merged into wider problems of politics, for it was during this period that France and England began to take an active part in Iberian politics. And lastly, as a result of this external interference, these years give us a first glimpse of John of Gaunt being initiated into a world that was for so long a time to play a large part in his dreams. But it is time to recall some of the details that justify these generalisations.

When Alfonso XI, King of Castile, died in 1349, his son Peter ascended the throne. Unfortunately for him, the sins of his father took very tangible shape in the persons of five illegitimate sons. It is not necessary to remember the names of all of them, but one, Henry of Trastamara, does not allow himself to be ignored, for he was to be a leading figure in Castilian history for some years. When the new king came to power, the illegitimate line naturally became the victims of the hates and fears of the legitimate line. Whoever murdered the mother Leonor (and blame has been distributed amongst several), the responsibility settled ultimately, as it was bound to do, upon Peter, who was then but a youth. He has lived in history as Peter the Cruel, a title that in late years has been subject to scrutiny. Those who would tilt a lance in his defence have suggested that he was no worse than his contemporaries. Perhaps not, but he was certainly no better, and when all has been said on his behalf, there remain some blemishes upon his character that explain the nickname he has borne. There is no need to linger over all of them ; but some affect our problem, for they created some of his greatest difficulties. Three days after his marriage in 1353 to Blanche of Bourbon, Peter deserted her for a former mistress, Maria de Padilla, a lady not without influence in later politics. Peter's action was, to say the least of it, lacking in tact, for Blanche was the sister-in-law of the king of France. Again, it was not long before Peter was involved in disputes with his neighbour, the king of Aragon. The sequel might have been prophesied. A man with a grievance soon had support. Before very long Henry of Trastamara was working hand in glove with the king of Aragon, and by 1363 was a pretender for Peter's throne. Provided with forces of German, Gascon and English adventurers, the famous White Companies, under French leadership and with papal encouragement, Henry was soon at war. In 1365 he entered Catalonia, and marched to Calahorra. Peter's opposition was futile, and his opponent was soon in possession of the country. At Burgos on 5th April, 1366, he was proclaimed king. Peter fled to Seville and eventually made for Corunna.

The stage was set for higher politics. Castilian affairs were no longer merely the concern of dwellers in the Peninsula. They had become important enough to affect other powerful interests. The Hundred Years War had passed through its first stage, but the Peace of Bretigny was an uneasy settlement. Neither side had any illusions. Each was on the watch for help in future times of trouble, so what had occurred in Castile mattered greatly. French support for Trastamara meant a friend for France on the Castilian throne. English possessions in France might well be endangered by these rapprochements.

Thus Peter, arrived at Corunna, had some reasons for supposing that the English might be interested in his plight. He appealed to the Black Prince who was at Bordeaux, and events proved his calculations correct. In response to his appeal the Black Prince sent help, and received him hospitably at Bordeaux. The council in England approved his action, and by September, plans were being discussed for an invasion of Castile in defence of the exile Peter. John of Gaunt was sent to England to raise troops, and in November he left with 400 men at arms and 600 archers. The campaign which followed belongs to the biography of the Black Prince rather than to John of Gaunt's story, although the latter played an active part in the military operations. For some, undoubtedly, the interesting figure in this episode is neither John of Gaunt, nor the Black Prince, nor yet Henry of Trastamara. It is the figure of the king of Navarre that lives in the memory. His territory was the key position in the invasion. Henry of Trastamara bribed him to shut his country against the Black Prince. Then the Black Prince bribed him to feed the English army while it passed through his dominions. And then, as a precautionary measure, the king of Navarre caused himself to be taken prisoner by the troops of the king of Aragon in order to avoid all his responsibilities. The Black Prince's victory at Najera in April, 1367 was another triumph in his military career, and meant the restoration of Peter to his throne. On the other hand, the use Peter made of his opportunity does not increase one's respect for his statesmanship. The cruelties he inflicted on those enemies who fell into his hands shocked the Black Prince, the ingratitude he showed in his efforts to avoid paying his debts to his supporters led to disputes, and at last the Black Prince withdrew to France, leaving Peter to get on as best he could.

Thus, by 1367 the first phase ended with two highly significant results. In the first place, during these seventeen years Castilian politics were brought into the main stream of European affairs. The fortunes of that country were now closely involved in the calculations of the powers engaged in the Hundred Years War. And, in the second place, these years had given John of Gaunt his first contact with the Peninsula. The next phase (1367-71) was to give him something more.

It was concerned in the main with John of Gaunt, for during those years there occurred some incidents which fixed once and for all his relation to Iberian problems. At the opening of the period John of Gaunt was a young man of twenty-seven, who had by nature of his position been given opportunities for advancement and experience. When he was two years old his father had made him Earl of Richmond. At an early age, as we have seen, he had been introduced to military life and had accompanied the Black Prince to the French Wars. As he grew older he acquired estates. In 1359, at the age of nineteen, he was married to Blanche, daughter and co-heiress of Henry, duke of Lancaster, and in 1362, after the death of his father-in-law, Edward III created him duke of Lancaster. He was the holder of the richest inheritance in the country. Already by 1367 he was playing an active part in government affairs, and had widened his knowledge of men and countries. But, so far as we can tell, he had not as yet found himself. He does not appear to have had any very clear goal in sight. The main interest of the years 1367-1371 lies in the fact that they provided him with an ambition, gave him an objective towards which he might strive, made him a man with a mission in life. To know what that objective was, and how he came to see it, we must recall other features of this second period.

As we look back upon John of Gaunt's career, we can hardly avoid the conviction that the really crucial year in it was 1369, for two events then occurred that were vital for his future. They were both of them deaths. The first was that of his wife Blanche. The second was that of Peter the Cruel. The first, as we shall see, made it possible for the second to affect John of Gaunt very closely.

When the Black Prince was restoring Peter to his throne, Henry of Trastamara had fled to Toulouse where he was soon busy avenging himself on his chief enemy by ravaging Aquitaine in the absence of the Black Prince. Frightened away by the appearance of that warrior, Henry of Trastamara betook himself once again to Castile. Here he found a favourable field. Many were already tired of Peter; there was an opening for a rival. So in 1368 Henry began an offensive by a march on Toledo. Gradually he was joined by French knights, always ready for a fight. In March, 1369, Peter attempted to drive him away from Toledo. He was routed, and took refuge in the castle of Montiel. The sequel was melodrama. Peter attempting to escape was captured and imprisoned in a tent. Here his enemy Trastamara visited him. Argument led to blows and the upshot was the death of Peter the Cruel.

Peter, at Bordeaux in 1366, had with him his two daughters, Constance and Isabella, the children of that Maria de Padilla for whom Peter had deserted Blanche of Bourbon. Now, these girls would have cut less of a figure in history had it not been that Peter maintained the priority of his marriage to Maria over that of his marriage to Blanche. If that priority be accepted, then it follows that the lawful heir to Peter's throne should have been Maria's son, Alfonso. But that young man had died in 1367, so on the death of Peter in 1369, his daughters Constance and Isabella inherited Alfonso's claim. If the legal arguments in support of this claim seem open to question, let us remember that there was someone who considered it worth a risk. In 1371 the widower, John of Gaunt, married Constance at Rocquefort. His brother, the earl of Cambridge, married Isabella.

One of the difficulties of mediæval history is the relative lack of those state papers, private letters, diaries, and similar intimate materials which, in later times, make plain the cross-purposes, the dreams, the ambitions and the motives of those who make history. We have no evidence that will enable us to analyse the ideas which led John of Gaunt to this marriage. We have to be content with the guesses suggested by events. But of one thing we may be reasonably sure. Henceforth the Duke of Lancaster had a mission. He would work for the recovery of the Castilian throne. He and his wife should be sovereigns *de jure*, no matter what usurper held the throne. So John of Gaunt from this point uses the title King of Castile, and makes his plans. Thus he passes into the third phase, to plan and plot, and wait, and work until the time should be ripe for him to risk all.

We, too, must pass on into that third phase. It is not an easy period. Events are unruly; they will not lend themselves to clear arrangement. Yet the landmarks we need can be seen if we regard the period as the time when the three main factors with which we have been dealing begin to come together. Two of them, Castile and John of Gaunt we know. But what of Portugal ?

If little has, as yet, been said about Portuguese politics, it is not because they were lacking in interest ; but earlier efforts to win independence belong to the general political history of the Iberian peninsula rather than to the story of Anglo-Portuguese relations. That those efforts had implanted in the people a fierce jealousy of outside interference, and a hostility to Castile is undoubtedly true, but from 1357-1367, Portuguese affairs scarcely affect the Castilian episode for the simple reason that Peter I of Portugal had the sense to refrain from interfering in the quarrel between Peter the Cruel and Henry of Trastamara. From 1367-1383, however, Portuguese policy took a very different course. The new King Ferdinand had his qualities, but he was weak, foolish, faithless and found it impossible to follow his predecessor's policy. He must needs meddle in Castilian affairs. What was worse, he does not seem to have known his own mind on these matters, with the result that he followed no consistent policy of aggression, but swayed weakly from one extreme to the opposite. Some examples will best illustrate his vacillations, and will show how his indecisions affected both his country and John of Gaunt.

On the death of Peter the Cruel, Ferdinand claimed the throne of Castile. This naturally strengthened the hand of Henry of Trastamara. Ferdinand found an ally in the king of Aragon, but he soon lost him because of his own treachery. Then he tried to get the English to do his work for him. John of Gaunt saw in the monarch who held Oporto and Lisbon, and who was an enemy to Castile, a friend who would let him in on the Castilian frontier, and from 1371 onwards there was a steady flow of communications between England and Portugal with the object of fixing an alliance. In November, 1372, John and Constance under the title of King and Queen of Castile made a treaty with Ferdinand and Leonora, King and Queen of Portugal, against the house of Trastamara. But in 1374 Ferdinand was actually lending the king of Castile ships for the use of the French against the English. In 1379 when Henry of Trastamara died, Ferdinand thought he saw his chance, so he was ready to renew the English alliance. If the Earl of Cambridge would come to Portugal with a thousand men at arms and an equal number of archers Ferdinand would help him to invade Castile. In 1381 the expedition was sent, thanks to the energetic wire-pulling of John of Gaunt. There is no story to tell of a brilliant military enterprise. On the contrary, the affair was a fiasco, due partly to the fact that the Earl of Cambridge was not the most brilliant of leaders, partly because he was inadequately equipped, but mostly because Ferdinand did not support him. The truth is not easy to gauge. Ferdinand's defence was that he had been deceived. He had expected that the expedition would be led by John of Gaunt in person. As he had not come, Ferdinand felt justified in coming to terms with Castile. He arranged a marriage alliance between his daughter Beatrice and the second son of the King of Castile.

That arrangement was to lead Ferdinand's subjects into deep waters. Just at the right moment in 1382 the queen of Castile died. Her husband modified the treaty, and married Beatrice himself. The terms of the marriage treaty suggest that Ferdinand and his draftsmen hardly appreciated what they were doing, for it is hard to believe that any Portuguese statesmen could have imagined they would succeed in persuading their countrymen to acquiesce. As though he wanted to put his subjects to the test, Ferdinand died soon afterwards, and when the king of Castile assumed the title to Ferdinand's throne the Portuguese took measures for meeting the situation. They found a leader and regent in an illegitimate son of Peter I, one John, Master of the Military Order of Avis. The domestic history of Portugal does not concern us here save in so far as it explains John of Gaunt. If it did, we should not lightly pass over one of those heroic occasions in the history of a people where they fight for freedom. We should have to dwell on the Battle of Aljubarota (14th August, 1385), where Portugal vindicated its independence and inflicted a blow to the military and political prestige of Castile from which that state did not recover for a considerable period. And in our account of the battle we should be permitted to note that not a few English volunteers fought on the Portuguese side. But all that is another story. For us this decisive period of Portuguese history is only significant because it had its reaction upon John of Gaunt. There was no sentiment in his response. He was not, so far as we can tell, fired by any enthusiasm for the Portuguese cause. Opportunism alone will explain his actions. According to one English contemporary it was this Portuguese victory that inspired him to open his attack on the Castilian throne. And we may well believe it. Conditions in the Peninsula were favourable. Castile was weak. In John of Avis, now king of Portugal he had a man more likely to be a support than Ferdinand would have been. Further, there were signs that it might be possible to tempt Richard II to lend a hand. In a word, by 1386, John of Gaunt's long awaited hour had struck. He was ready to lead an expedition into Spain.

The support he needed he obtained from two very different quarters. The first, very naturally, was Richard II. Having made an agreement with that monarch, which included a loan of money, John saw Richard ready to make a treaty with Portugal, and in May, 1386 the famous treaty of Windsor was arranged. It is the great landmark in Anglo-Portuguese relations, but we cannot do more than summarise its main clauses. Briefly they may be stated to include a perpetual league between the two countries, whereby each was to assist the other against all enemies, a refusal by each party to help the enemies of the other, a safe conduct to all subjects of the one party within the territories of the other, and a condition of confirmation by future rulers of each country.

The other quarter from which support came will not, perhaps, be so obvious. It was Pope Urban VI. His policy is an illuminating sidelight on the tangled web of fourteenth century politics in Europe. These were the years of the Great Schism, when two popes struggled for supremacy and it is natural to find that controversy reflected in the politics of all the states with which we are dealing. England was in favour of Urban VI, seeing in Clement VII a friend of the French. Portugal, under English influence, came over to Urban's side. It need hardly be said that Castile supported Clement, so when John of Gaunt planned his expedition, Urban saw a way of doing himself a good turn. Papal bulls raised the expedition into a crusade against a schismatic. It was all to the good so far as recruiting men and money went ; but as a crusade the expedition was not a success. Only one recorded incident gives colour to John of Gaunt's attitude. When he reached Santiago, one of the first things he did was to turn out the archbishop, a follower of Clement, and put in his place a supporter of Urban. Then real politics seem to have made him forgetful of this aspect of his expedition. We hear no more of the crusade.

With the arrival of John of Gaunt in the Peninsula in July 1386, we enter on the final stage of his adventure. What are we to make of this long planned effort to win a crown in a foreign land ? If history were a straightforward exercise in accountancy, we should be able to present a balanced statement. But I cannot resist the fancy that more often than not in the affairs of men two and two do not make four. Take, for example, the case before us. By all the laws of commonsense, John of Gaunt's accounts ought to be showing a heavy deficit. And yet, do they ? Let us look at them a little more closely, beginning where every wise man who wants to know the worst would begin, with the debit side. There is, indeed, a formidable list of items.

Firstly, we ought to notice that he set out on a military expedition, the object of which was the conquest and occupation of Castile. That objective was not reached. From a military point of view his expedition was a complete failure. He landed in the Peninsula on the 25th July, 1386. He left for Bayonne, all fighting over, in November, 1387. What did these months do for his cause and for his reputation as a soldier ? There was some aimless marching to and fro in Galicia, a few nominal sieges, no serious battles, and certainly no great victories. His troops went from town to town announcing the arrival of the lawful king and queen of the country, and calling upon subjects to receive them. For the most part the people were listless. They were not interested in the politics of the question. Meanwhile the Duke's troops were open to attacks of disease, and were being depleted for garrison purposes. Then there was a more serious attempt at a military campaign in Leon in March, 1387, when John of Gaunt had received support from Portugal. Even this was not impressive. The English troops were by this time suffering severely from sickness, and what was more important, the enemy could not be found. The king of Castile sedulously refused pitched battle. How could there be a decisive victory when there was no-one with whom to fight ? So much, then, for the value of the military operations.

The second item in the debit account needs only a few words. John of Gaunt set out with the object of making himself and Constance king and queen of Castile in fact as well as in right. When all was over, John was still John of Gaunt, Duke of Lancaster, and his opponent was still king of Castile.

The third item in the debit account is the disillusion that marked the end of John's dreams. For years he had persuaded himself of a destiny that would make him king of Castile, and a powerful agent to support England against the French. Contact with reality showed that in the achievement of these plans the people of the Peninsula counted. Though Castile and Portugal might take sides in the dynastic rivalries of their respective countries, neither of them would, in the last resort, tolerate the imposition of a foreigner as king, least of all when he owed his success to the support of its rival. If John of Gaunt had ideas that he might get support from Castilians, his expedition showed he was wrong. He was trying to win a crown in a country which would not accept outside intervention in its politics.

When we have listed these facts it does not seem possible to find much to put on the credit side. And yet we have not finished with this expedition. There is more in it than that. Look in the first place at the diplomatic side of the venture. However disappointing the military events appear, John of Gaunt's handling of diplomacy does him no discredit. He came to the Peninsula not very sure of his reception by the Portuguese. In about a month, before he was much wiser, he was confronted by a Castilian embassy which —when all the cards were on the table—revealed that their king was prepared to compromise on the basis of a marriage between the heir of Castile and the heiress of John and Constance. In the absence of documentary evidence we have a choice in interpreting John of Gaunt's answer. We may hold that he was confident of victory and so would not compromise. Or we may be ready to allow him credit for finer feelings, suggesting that he was too honourable to make an agreement before he knew what his Portuguese ally thought. Whichever view we take, the importance of the decision he made cannot be doubted. The rejection of the Castilian terms strengthened the relations between the King of Portugal and John of Gaunt. Each began to learn that the other could be trusted. And John of Avis showed that he could respond. At Ponte do Mouro in November, 1386, he agreed to support John of Gaunt, and arranged to marry the Duke's daughter Philippa. He showed his sagacity in avoiding her sister Catherine, for her rights to the Castilian throne would have brought trouble to his country. As it was, he brought into his court a Lancastrian queen, and so linked the destinies of Portugal and England. In the sequel John of Avis played his part, and when in March, 1387, he and his English ally met at Braganza to begin an invasion of Castile, it was clear that Portugal intended to interpret the terms of the agreement generously.

Thus, the friendship with Portugal, forged by the sympathy and unofficial support the English had given to the Portuguese in their struggle for autonomy, strengthened by the Treaty of Windsor, and confirmed by the experience of John of Gaunt in his transactions with John of Avis, was an abiding contribution to the story of Anglo-Portuguese relations. There were advantages for both countries. From then on, throughout the fifteenth century, the two countries are found working together, and their common interests are catered for in several important treaties. Such a relationship was something bigger than an alliance for concerted action against Castile. For both countries it implied more than an agreement on a question of foreign politics. It touched more vital realities.

In the study of Anglo-Portuguese relations the cross-currents of politics and diplomacy should not occupy the mind to the exclusion of all else. Side by side with the calculations of claimants to thrones must be placed the humbler, more prosaic, but more essential schemes of purveyors of wines, figs, grapes, spices, wax, leather, silk, cork, wool and cloth. These commodities, and the men who trafficked in them, played a larger part than a John of Gaunt probably dreamed. In touching upon these things we are opening a subject that at first sight may seem to be a digression ; but it is at least arguable that such an opinion is incorrect. Admittedly it is with some hesitation that most of us would include economic policy on the credit side of John of Gaunt's account. If it is to go there at all it must be as unearned increment, for economic policy as such seems to have had little if any place in his schemes. All the same, his achievements were not without influence in affairs of trade and they cannot be dismissed until we have suggested whither they were to lead.

Trading relations between England and Portugal go

back to the early thirteenth century when Portuguese merchants are to be found in England. With the fourteenth century, their position steadily became more secure until, by the time of Edward III, they gained privileges sufficient to enable them to carry on trade without much hindrance. They were capable of looking after their own interests, and in 1353, after the English and Portuguese kings had failed to carry through a projected marriage alliance, the Portuguese merchants made a highly interesting commercial treaty with Edward III. For success in their enterprises peace between the two countries was essential and the fact that John of Gaunt helped to produce such conditions made his activities of some consequence to trade. The economic effects of the Hundred Years War modified the trading problem. As a result of the war, the English lost their hold on the vineyards of Gascony, and French interference, together with the troubled relations with Castile, made wine difficult to obtain. Thus the market for Portuguese wine in England was good. On the other hand, English merchants found in Portugal a growing market for their cloth. As the fifteenth century developed, trade between the two countries increased. Early in the century two Bristol customs accounts mention only wines of Gascony and Spain. In 1465-1466 six ships came from Portugal into that port with nearly 500 tuns of wine, and as time went on, that trade expanded. There were similar developments in the trade in cork, sugar, salt, wax and olive oil.

How far did the work of the diplomatists assist ? Statesmen were not blind to the problem, and clauses in the treaty of Windsor embodied the wishes of the merchants of both countries for protection for trade. It cannot be said that the treaty was immediately beneficial to the Portuguese. Trade flowed in the direction of the English merchants. They were favoured in Portugal. Privileges hitherto enjoyed there solely by the merchants of Genoa and Pisa were extended to them, and special arrangements gave them such advantages that by the middle of the fifteenth century, Portuguese merchants were complaining that the English were more favourably placed for trade in Portugal than were the natives. On the other hand, their own position in England was not so happy. After the middle of the fifteenth century, however, the treaty of Windsor tended to be more closely observed. Petitions of Portuguese merchants show by their repeated references to it that they regarded its clauses as important privileges and it was confirmed by the Yorkist kings.

That all this was due to John of Gaunt it would be folly to assert. What can be said is that trade was assisted by peace. That is why the history of Anglo-Portuguese commercial relations in the fourteenth and fifteenth centuries were far more satisfactory than those of England and Castile during the same period. Inasmuch as the treaty of Windsor grew out of the Peninsula politics of John of Gaunt he is entitled to some recognition, even though it be of the kind that belongs to one who knew not what he did.

Returning to his accounts, there is yet one item to be placed to his credit. In diplomacy the arrangement with Portugal was not his only victory. He shows to good advantage in his dealings with the king of Castile. That monarch was determined not to fight, and when the decimation of John of Gaunt's forces by disease made it impossible for the Anglo-Portuguese offensive to be continued, Castilian ambassadors brought again an offer of peace. The terms were the same as they had been at the beginning of the venture, but this time John of Gaunt felt he had better accept them. In

October, 1387 he withdrew to Bayonne and awaited the arrival of the Castilian ambassadors to draw up the details.

Even here he showed a master touch. The ambassadors were slow in putting in an appearance so John of Gaunt took a hand. Knowing that relations between Castile and France were strained, he gave out that he was negotiating a French marriage for Catherine. When the news reached Castile, there was anxiety and the treaty was soon an accomplished fact. An examination of its clauses adds considerably to our respect for the Duke, for when we remember the futility of his military operations, it is really astonishing that he should have won such good terms. True, he and his wife agreed to transfer to the King of Castile all the rights they claimed to the Castilian throne; but all was not lost. The succession question was settled by a proposed marriage between the eldest son of King John (a lad of ten named Henry) and the daughter of John of Gaunt (a girl of fourteen, named Catherine). They were to be heirs to the Castilian throne, provided with an estate suitable to their position. John of Gaunt was taking no risks. It was agreed that the King of Castile's second son, Ferdinand, should remain unmarried until after his brother's marriage to Catherine had been celebrated, so as to be available in case his brother died before the event could take place. And if the worst were to happen, and all John of Castile's children were to die without issue, there was to be yet one more arrangement. The crown of Castile was then to revert to the children of Constance and John of Gaunt. That last eventuality did not occur. The marriage of Catherine and Henry introduced the Lancastrian line into Castilian history.

There were other, more tangible, satisfactions for the Duke of Lancaster, including an annuity of 40,000 gold francs paid, apparently, almost up to his death, and an indemnity of 600,000 gold francs payable at Bayonne in two equal instalments within the next three years.

On the whole, then, it is fair to see in John of Gaunt's relations with the Peninsula something more than the folly of an ambitious man. It was an enterprise by no means lacking in historical importance. Contemporaries were impressed by his success, and a member of his suite gossiped proudly of the sight he saw when a train of 47 mules heavily laden with chests full of gold brought the second instalment of the indemnity to John of Gaunt at Bayonne. But what were the emotions of the Duke at that moment? Was he thinking a little wistfully of those two golden crowns?

Bibliography.

English readers will find general bibliographies for the history of the Iberian Peninsula in *The Cambridge Mediæval History*, Vols, VI, 912-22 ; VII, 919-31. The essential modern book on the life of John of Gaunt and his relations with the Peninsula is S. Armitage-Smith, *John of Gaunt* (London, 1904), a well-documented, full-length biography to which all later writers must be heavily indebted. It contains a bibliography.

For the background of Iberian politics, readers should consult *The Cambridge Mediæval History*, VII, c. 20 ; Chapman, C. E., *A History of Spain* (New York, 1918) ; Merriman, R. B., *The Rise of the Spanish Empire in the Old World and the New*, Vol. I (New York, 1918). For English politics during the period, the following will be found useful : Oman, C., *The Political History of England*, 1377-1485; *The Cambridge Mediæval History*, VII, c. 15 ; Longman, W., *The Life and Times of Edward III*. Some papers and monographs dealing with special aspects of the problem are : Daumet, G., *Etude sur l'alliance de la France et de la Castile au XIVe et au XVe siecles* (Bibl. de l'ecole des Hautes Etudes, 118, 1898), *Etudes sur les relations d'Innocent IV avec D. Pedro I, Roi de Castile au sujet de Blanche de Bourbon* (1897), and *Memoire sur les relations de la France et de la Castile*, 1255-1320 (Paris, 1913) ; Déprez, E., *La bataille de Najera* (Rev. hist., 136, 1921. 37-59) ; Guichot, J., D. *Pedro Primero de Castilla* (Seville, 1878); Mérimée, P., *Histoire de Don Pedre 1er roi de Castile* (Paris, 1865) ; Oman, C., *Art of War in the Middle Ages*, II (London, 1924) ; Shillington, V. M., *The Beginnings of the Anglo-Portuguese Alliance* (Trans. Royal Hist. Soc., N.S., XX, 109-132) ; Shillington, V. M. and Chapman, A. B. W., *Commercial Relations of England and Portugal* (London, 1907) ; Wilson, M. Carus., *The Overseas Trade of Bristol* in *English Trade in the Fifteenth Century* (ed. E. Power and M. Postan, London, 1933) ; Prestage, E., *The Anglo-Portuguese Alliance* (Trans. Royal Hist. Soc., 4th S., xvii, 69-100).

The original authorities are listed in Armitage-Smith, *op. cit.* From the English side, the chief narratives are : *Chronicon Henrici Knighton* (ed. J. R. Lumby, Rolls Series) ; *Chronicon Angliæ* (ed. E. M. Thompson, Rolls Series) ; *Eulogium Historiarum* (ed. E. S. Haydon, Rolls Series) ; *Polychronicon Ranulphi Higden* (VIII, IX, ed. J. Lumby, Rolls Series). On the Portuguese side the principal source is *Chronica de El Rei D. João I*, by Fernão Lopes (Bibl. de Classicos Portuguezes, Lisbon, 1897). For extracts in English translation, and an illuminating account of the chronicler, see Prestage, E., *The Chronicles of Fernão Lopes and Gomes Eannes de Zurara* (1928). The most important diplomatic documents will be found in Rymer, *Foedera*, (1704), Vol. VII.

CHAPTER III.

Anglo-Portuguese Rivalry in the Persian Gulf, 1615-1635.

Some explanation is perhaps needed as to why this particular subject should have been selected as the topic for this paper. When Professor Prestage asked me to contribute something on the Asiatic aspect of Anglo-Portuguese relations, I rather unthinkingly accepted the proposal, without having any precise idea of what subject to choose. In actual fact, the field of choice is more limited than might be supposed, for after the first armed clashes between the two nations in the Indian seas were over, the story of their mutual relations is mainly a hum-drum and uneventful one ; the almost unbroken peace which prevailed between them after the treaty of 1635, being marred only by a few scuffles in the vicinity of Bombay Harbour, or by an acrimonious exchange of notes over the vexed question of the delimitation of the boundary lands and islands near Bombay and Bassein. The more obvious aspects of Anglo-Portuguese relations in the East, such as the acquisition of Bombay in 1661-1665, or the rather sorry part played by the English in the disastrous Mahratta war against the Portuguese in 1737-1741, have already been dealt with adequately by more than one competent historian. Nor for that matter has the story of Anglo-Portuguese rivalry in the Persian Gulf been unduly neglected, but the tale has been told almost entirely from the English side, whereas I propose to deal with it more from the point of view of the men " on the other side of the hill." Fortunately the telling of it is enlivened by more than one stirring incident, for that element of romance which seems to be inseparable from the early Stuart adventurers is equally to be found in their Lusitanian opponents ; so that the story of their rivalry is something more than a mere echo of " old, unhappy, far-off things and battles long ago."

It may be as well to state here briefly, the principal sources on which this paper is based. There is no lack of material, whether printed or manuscript, on the English side, and to all intents and purposes the student will find everything he wants to know printed in two works, both of them exemplary monuments of patient research. I refer to Samuel Purchas' *Pilgrimes*, of which the best edition is that originally published at London in 1625 (reprinted, Glasgow, 1905) and to Sir William Foster's series on *The English Factories in India* of which the relevant volumes are the five covering the years 1618-1636, printed at Oxford, 1906-1911. To these may be added Mr. Noel Sainsbury's painstaking compilation of the *Calendar of State Papers, Colonial Series, East Indies*, for the years 1615-1634 (London, 1862-1892), though this work has been largely superseded by Sir William Foster's scholarly volumes.

On the Portuguese side, we have nothing to compare in fullness and accuracy with the English sources. The *Documentos remettidos da India* or *Books of the Monsoons*, published by the Lisbon Academy of Sciences in four volumes (Lisboa, 1880-1893) cover the second decade of the seventeenth century, but are not nearly so helpful as might be expected. The series contains all the letters from the home authorities to the Indian government at Goa during the period in question, but has very few letters sent by the Portuguese officials in Asia to their superiors in Europe, which would be of far greater value and interest to us. More enlightening, as also more entertaining, are the piquant memoirs of a Spanish *hidalgo*, Don Garcia de Silva y Figueroa, who was Ambassador from the King of Spain to Shah Abbas the Great, in the eventful years preceding the siege and capture of Ormuz. Don Garcia had a pen dipped in vinegar and no great love for his Portuguese fellow-subjects,[1] so it is not surprising that there is no Portuguese edition of his diary. The original manuscript was first published in full under the title of *Commentarios*, in two volumes, printed at Madrid in 1903, but as early as 1667, a French translation had been made by Abraham de Wicquefort and published at Paris.

Naturally enough, the siege of Ormuz in 1622 bulks largely in contemporary literature, forming as it does the turning-point in the struggle for power between English and Portuguese in the Gulf. The military and naval operations before, during and immediately after the siege, are fully dealt with in the *Commentarios do grande Capitão Ruy Freyre de Andrade*, originally printed at Lisbon in 1647, and of which an annotated English translation was published at London in 1929. This work, although based upon contemporary papers and despatches, is not as reliable as it should have been, owing to the arbitrary way in which the original editor-publisher, Lourenço Craesbeeck, used his material. Still, the more important errors and omissions can be readily detected by comparison with the contemporary English accounts, as reproduced by Purchas and Foster. A further check upon the *Commentarios* is afforded by a

[1]It will be remembered that from 1580-1640, Spain and Portugal formed a dual monarchy under a single King.

little work edited at Lisbon in 1641 by Luiz Marinho de Azevedo and entitled *Apologeticos Discursos em defensa da fama e boa memoria de Fernão de Albuquerque, Governador que foi da India, contra o que d'elle escreveu D. Gonsalo de Cespedes, na Chronica d'El Rei D. Filippe IV de Castella.* As its title implies, this little book was published to vindicate the conduct of Fernão de Albuquerque, who was Governor of India from 1619-1622, and who did not always see eye to eye with Ruy Freyre, although he loyally supported him during his campaigns against the Persians and English in the Gulf. Although not so detailed as the *Commentarios,* it is often more reliable, and has never yet been used by any modern writer on the subject. Upon the 1647 edition of the *Commentarios,* Snr. Luciano Cordeiro, the indefatigable secretary of the Lisbon Geographical Society, based his *Como se perdeu Ormuz* (Lisboa, 1896). Although the learned author treated Lourenço Craesbeeck's compilation with greater respect than it deserves, he atoned for his uncritical acceptation of the former's patriotic embellishments, by printing as an appendix to his own work, a large number of contemporary documents on the siege of Ormuz which are of the greatest value and interest. Snr. Cordeiro followed up his first book with a small publication entitled *Dois Capitães da India* (Lisboa, 1898) which contains several documents narrating in detail the progress of Portuguese arms in the Persian Gulf during the years 1623-1629, thus forming a continuation of the Ormuz operations. Another valuable mine of information for this period is the *Travels* of that "cultured Roman," Pietro della Valle. This learned voyager travelled up the Gulf in 1625, and the narrative of his voyage throws numerous sidelights on the chief personages and events concerned. An English edition of his *Travels* was printed at London in 1665, and re-edited for the Hakluyt Society by Mr. Edward Grey in 1891. Printed sources in Portuguese for the years 1625-1635 are singularly few and far between, being practically limited to a few paragraphs in the third volume of Faria y Sousa's not too trustworthy *Asia Portuguesa* (Lisbon, 1675) and some incidental notices in rare missionary tracts, such as the *Carta do Padre Vigairo da ordem de St. Agostinho* etc. (Lisboa, 1628). An exception is formed by the narratives of the three hard fought battles in the Persian Gulf, between an Anglo-Dutch squadron and a Portuguese armada under Nuno Alvarez Botelho, in February, 1625 ; these fights produced quite a spate of pamphlet literature on the subject in Portuguese, Spanish, Dutch and English, one of the latter tracts being edited by John Taylor, the Water-Poet. Later and partly traditional accounts of the Ormuz operations, such as those given by Father Queiroz in his *Historia da vida do venerauel irmão Pedro de Basto*, (Lisboa, 1689), are worth only a passing mention.

The amount of relevant material to be found in Portuguese archives is disappointingly small, most of the contemporary documents and reports having perished in the great fire which destroyed the building in which they were housed, the *Casa da India*, after the disastrous Lisbon earthquake of 1755; whilst the white ant has been responsible for the destruction of many old documents in the Goa archives. The scarcity of material in Portugal, is however compensated for to some extent, (at least as concerns the Ormuz operations) by a large number of contemporary Portuguese letters and reports preserved amongst the Egerton manuscripts in the British Museum. These have not been consulted by historians up till now, and should not be neglected by any future writer on the subject.

All or most of the foregoing sources deal with wars

and rumours of wars, but the commercial activities of the Portuguese in the Persian Gulf during the period under review, are adequately dealt with by Antonio Bocarro, the official Chronicler of Portuguese India from 1631-1643, a contemporary copy of whose monumental *Livro do Estado da India Oriental* is to be found in the Sloane Library at the British Museum. In this exhaustive review of the geographical, political and economic situation of the Portuguese possessions in Asia, which was completed at Goa in 1635, Bocarro gives a detailed description of the Portuguese settlements and agencies at Muscat, Kung, Basra and all other places frequented by the Lusitanians in the Gulf. Some of these (e.g., those on Ormuz and Basra) were reproduced by W. de Gray Birch in the Hakluyt Society edition of the *Commentarios* of Affonso de Albuquerque (London, 1880). The maps and plans of the various fortresses which accompany the descriptions, are also of considerable interest, although their artistic value is small.[1]

---

[1]Antonio Bocarro was born at Abrantes in 1594, his brother being the celebrated physician and writer, Manoel Bocarro Francez. The family was of Israelite origin, and Antonio Bocarro, after sailing to India in 1622, first settled in the Jewish community at Cochim. In 1624 he was a prisoner of the Inquisition at Goa, but was appointed the official historian by the Conde de Linhares (well-known as a protector of the *Christãos-novos*) in 1631. Mr. de Gray Birch and several other English writers err in ascribing Bocarro's *magnum opus* to Pedro Barreto de Rezende, private secretary of the Conde de Linhares who was Viceroy of India from 1629-1635. Rezende did in fact co-operate in the work, but he explicitly states in the prologue that he was responsible only for the actual plans of the fortresses, the whole of the text having been drawn up by Antonio Bocarro. The British Museum copy, which is a later one of about 1646, includes some interesting hydrographic charts of Asiatic waters from the pen of Pierre Berthelot, a Norman who first came to the Indies as pilot of a French ship in 1619. In later years he rose to be Pilot and Cosmographer-major of India in the Portuguese service, and after becoming a Carmelite monk was martyred in Achin in 1638. Contemporary copies of Antonio Bocarro's work exist in Evora and Paris ; whilst others are mentioned by the Portuguese bibliographer, Barbosa Machado, in Vol. I of his *Bibliotheca Lusitana*. Bocarro's original preface is dated Goa, 17th February, 1635 and Pedro Barreto de Rezende's copy in The British Museum, *Anno de* 1646.

51

So much for the principal English and Portuguese sources, but it must not be forgotten that it is often the looker-on who sees most of the game. An interested onlooker, and at times active participant, was the "insolent Hollander" as his jealous English rivals often dubbed him, and it is from Dutch accounts that we can glean many facts which passed unnoticed, or were glossed over, by the parties directly concerned. For instance, a good deal of material is to be found in some of the journals printed in volume II of the *Begin ende Voortgangh der Vereenighde Oost-Indische Compagnie*, published at Amsterdam in 1646 ; particularly in that of Hendrik Hagenaer who travelled in the Gulf during the years 1632-1633. The voluminous *Dagh-Register gehouden int Casteel Batavia*, the modern publication of which (at Batavia and the Hague 1887-1912) corresponds roughly to Sir William Foster's *English Factories in India* series (albeit the former is edited in a far less scholarly way), contains a good deal of relevant material, although the diaries for some of the years concerned (e.g., 1630 and 1635) are unfortunately missing, either in whole or in part. Mr. A. Hotz's scholarly edition (Leyden, 1907) of the log-book of skipper Cornelis Roobacker, who charted a part of the Gulf during his voyage from Gombrun to Basra in 1645, is also worth consulting ; as is Dr. H. Terpstra's *De opkomst der Westerkwartieren van de Oost-Indische Compagnie* (The Hague, 1918)—another careful piece of research.

An even more deeply interested party in the spectacle of Anglo-Portuguese rivalry in the Gulf was the Persian himself. Unfortunately, being guiltless of any knowledge of the Iranian tongue, I cannot claim to have translated a mass of Persian and Arabic documents on the subject, and do not even know if such exist. If by any chance they do, it would be interesting to study them for the sake of getting an insight into their point of view ; but it is improbable that they would have much of importance to add to the voluminous English, Portuguese and Dutch accounts.

Finally, it should not be forgotten that nothing can quite supply the want of personal experience of the sea or land area under discussion. Nevertheless, although it is given to few of us to be able to travel there, yet a good idea of the geographical and climatic conditions obtaining in that desolate region, can be obtained from a consultation of such sources as Sir Arnold Wilson's standard work on *The Persian Gulf*, or of Admiralty charts and *The Persian Gulf Pilot*. It may be added that the series of aerial photographs published in *The Times* during 1934, affords us some excellent glimpses of the forbidding nature of the country in which Englishmen and " Portugals " fought out their quarrels three hundred years ago.

As early as 1612 the Portuguese began to take alarm at the prospect of their English rivals opening a trade with Persia, and thus interfering with their own monopoly of sea-borne commerce in the Gulf, which they had held practically unchallenged for a century. Although the English at this time had their hands full at Surat, whilst subsequently King James I's ambassador to the court of the Great Moghul, Sir Thomas Roe, opposed the extension of their trade to Persia, yet the activities of the celebrated adventurer, Robert Sherley, aroused considerable misgivings in the minds of the Lusitanian authorities at Lisbon and Goa. Accordingly when Sherley returned from his mission on behalf of Shah Abbas to the courts of London and Madrid in 1612, the Portuguese Indiamen which sailed for Goa in the same year, brought warning letters concerning his activities to Dom Hieronymo de Azevedo, the Viceroy at Goa.

These warnings were duplicated by others which were sent overland in the following year, and which reached Goa at the beginning of November, 1613. In these letters, the Viceroy was ordered to prevent by fair means or foul Dom Roberto, as he is termed in Portuguese documents, from reaching Persia ; and it was not the fault of Azevedo that his prey escaped him. As soon as these orders of the Lisbon authorities had been received in Goa, it was resolved to hasten the departure of Dom Luiz da Gama, who was about to proceed to take up the captaincy of the fortress of Ormuz ; and to give him a sufficient naval and military force to ensure his being able to secure Sherley's person by force if necessary. Da Gama was ordered to proceed forthwith to Laribandar (Diul-Sind) at the mouth of the Indus, where Sherley had been landed together with his companions from England in the *Expedition*, and to offer the local Governor a bribe of 6,000 *pardaus*, to induce him to surrender the intended victim ; failing which, he was to be offered an equally large bribe to kill him. Dom Hieronymo, in reporting this drastic decision to the home authorities, added that he felt sure that Dom Luiz da Gama would succeed in his mission, both because of his own capabilities, and because the Governor, like all Mohamedans, would be easily bribed, whilst Sherley had nothing to offer as a counter-bribe. Nevertheless, Sir Robert escaped the trap set for him, and Dom Luiz arrived off Sind in January, 1614 to find that the bird had flown. Sherley's principal companion, Sir Thomas Powell, the ambassador-elect from the " British Solomon " to Shah Abbas, together with several members of his entourage died, but he himself

54

managed to escape from the clutches of the local Indian authorities, and made his way to the court of Jahangir at Agra, whence he proceeded to Persia by way of Kandahar.[1]

Encouraged by Sherley's promises, and cheered by the news that " the King of Persia much favoureth the English nation, and is of late fallen out with the Portugals," the chief factors at Surat now resolved to try to open up a trade with Persia. The maritime power of the Portuguese had been greatly reduced since their disastrous defeats by the English off Swally in 1610, and again in January, 1615 ; whilst at the same time, their small fort at Gombrun which guarded the wells on the mainland whence the population and garrison of Ormuz depended for most of their water supply, was attacked and taken by the Khan of Lar, after a trifling resistance. All these events were of good augury for the East-India Company, and after a preliminary journey to Ispahan by two factors in 1615, the first English vessel destined for the Persian trade, the *James*, was despatched from Surat in 1616. The Portuguese attempt to intercept the vessel proved abortive, and after this first successful venture had been repeated in the two following years, a factory was definitely settled at Jask in 1619, which became the centre of the East India Company's commercial activities in Persia for the next three years.

It is interesting to note that one of the reasons which induced the Surat factors to embark on their Persian adventure in 1616, was the fact that Sherley was absent from Persia, having been sent by his master

[1] See the correspondence of Dom Hieronymo de Azevedo with his home Government on the question of intercepting Sherley, as printed by Cunha Rivara on pp. 207-211 of the *Chronista de Tissuary*, I, Nova Goa, 1866. *Cf* also Bocarro *Decada XIII*, pp. 201-203, and the journal of Sherley's voyage out to Sind in the *Expedition* as printed by Purchas in Vol. I of his *Pilgrimes* (1625 edition).

the Shah on another mission to the King of Spain early in the same year. Evidently the help he had so freely proffered three years earlier was found to have been rather expensive ; at any rate it was noted that if he had still been at the Shah's court, he would either have hindered the English in their enterprise, or " to our great charge as we suppose would lend us his furtherance." The presence of Sir Robert in Goa this year, as the honoured guest of the Viceroy who had done his utmost to have him poisoned or murdered a bare two years before, was certainly rather amusing. It will be remembered that although the Portuguese fortress of Ormuz was a thorn in the eye of Shah Abbas from the beginning of his reign, and that he had long since been determined to secure it, yet there was another even more powerful enemy, in the shape of the Turk, on his western frontier. It is true that with the capture of Nehavend and Tabriz, the Osmanali had been fairly driven out of the North-west Persian provinces by 1605, but the long-continued war with the Sultan seriously affected the Persian silk trade with Europe (largely a royal monopoly), which had either to pass overland through the domains of the Turkish enemies, or else by the sea-route controlled by the Portuguese. Shah Abbas' attitude towards the Lusitanians, depended almost entirely on the progress of his arms against the Turks, and any decisive success over the latter was usually followed by the adoption of a more openly hostile attitude towards the former. Thus in 1602 the valuable pearl fishery of Bahrein, off the north Arabian coast, had been forcibly seized from the feeble grasp of the puppet " King " of Ormuz who was a suzerain of the King of Spain. This aggression was followed up in 1607 and 1615 by the occupation of the wells and fort of Gombrun on which Ormuz largely depended for its supplies of fresh water ;

but the Turkish menace still prevented Shah Abbas from breaking openly with the Portuguese. Not only so, but he had frequently sent ambassadors to Madrid with proposals to the effect that in return for active Spanish assistance against the Turks in the Levant and elsewhere, he would give the Portuguese a monopoly of all the trade of Persia with Europe. This offer had been made at different times by such varied representatives as the Portuguese friar Antonio de Gouvea, the two Sherley brothers, Robert and Anthony, and by the native Persian ambassador Dengis Beg in 1608. The Spanish government for many years hesitated to accept this apparently alluring offer, as they fully realised that only the fear of the Turks had induced the Shah to make it at all; but in 1614, largely as a result of Robert Sherley's previous persuasions, it was decided to send an ambassador with power to conclude an agreement on these lines, provided that Bahrein and Gombrun were restored to the King of Ormuz. The envoy selected was a courtly old Spanish *hidalgo* named Don Garcia de Silva y Figeroa, and he embarked at Lisbon in April, 1614 with a large retinue and " an extraordinary rich present " for the Shah.[1] He arrived at Goa in November, but his reception by the local Portuguese authorities was none of the most cordial; and he likewise fell foul of Sherley who reached Goa in March 1616, on his way to Europe on a reciprocal mission to the court of Madrid. Shah Abbas' dilemma was well summed up by Sir Thomas Roe, who wrote that he must either " constantly resolve to go through

[1]It is amusing to note that the selection of Don Garcia as ambassador was the direct result of a request by the Shah that no more ecclesiastical envoys should be sent him, " as a Religious out of his cell is like a fish out of water." Della Valle also criticises the habit of the Portuguese of sending priests or friars as envoys to native princes, and adds that this practice merely brought them into disrepute. On the other hand, the custom may have been due in part to the fact that the priests (or at any rate the Jesuits) were usually skilled linguists.

with the Spaniard, or to make peace with the Turk ; one of them he must do." To most observers it seemed that Abbas had come down on the Spanish side of the fence, for when he sent Sherley on his new mission to Goa and Madrid in 1615, he was provided with fuller powers and instructions than before. In truth the Shah was only biding his time ; for whilst Sherley was negotiating a definite treaty of alliance in Madrid, he deliberately broke off all negotiations with Don Garcia de Silva at Ispahan, on the pretext that the Spanish demand for the restitution of Bahrein and Gombrun as a *sine qua non,* was totally unjustified. The real reason for his removing the mask, however, was that the appearance of English ships at Jask afforded him a welcome opportunity of disposing of the silks, through other hands than those of his actual or potential enemies.

The arrival of the English at Jask in 1616 and the subsequent foundation of the factory there, aroused the liveliest misgivings in the minds of the Portuguese authorities, which the bland professions of the Shah, or the persuasive eloquence of Robert Sherley could by no means entirely allay. Even whilst the embassy of Don Garcia de Silva was still treating with the Shah, measures were being taken by the home authorities to prepare for the worst, in the event of an agreement not being arrived at. It was fully realised that the English would not tamely abandon the trade they had successfully begun, and that the continuance of Portuguese political and commercial preponderance in the Gulf depended entirely on the maintenance of their supremacy at sea. It was therefore decided to despatch a strong naval force from Lisbon to Ormuz in the spring of 1619, with the dual object of forcibly ejecting the intruding English " corsairs," and of securing the fortress against a possible Persian attack.

It is a common if natural failing of English historians, that they tell us little or nothing about the men from whom our ancestors had to wrest the mastery of the seas, before they could enjoy the fruits of their " quiet trade " in peace. This is hardly surprising, since so many of the founders of our own colonial empire (outstanding figures like Robert Clive always excepted) have been unduly neglected, that it is only natural they should claim the first share of our attention. Of late years, however, the patient labours of Sir William Foster and other investigators, have restored to their rightful places such leading figures as Captain John Weddel and William Methwold, so that a few words about their principal opponents may not come amiss. It is impossible to apprise the deeds of the first Englishmen in India at their true worth, if we have no idea of what manner of men they were, against whom they had to fight for " the wealth of Ormuz and of Ind." It is easy to dismiss the lot of them as decadent " dagoes " or priest-ridden Papists, but in doing so we sadly under-rate the achievements of our fore-fathers. If all the opponents of the English in India during the seventeenth century had been as cowardly and as inefficient as they are commonly made out to be, then the foundation of our Indian Empire was neither a particularly onerous nor honourable task. Such, however, was not the case, and along with many weaklings and half-castes, the ranks of the Portuguese in India included soldiers and sailors who gave every bit as much as they received. " Who so cowardly as a Portuguese ? " asked Captain Downton sneeringly of his men before the fight in Swalley Hole ; but he had the fairmindedness to admit in his journal afterwards, that he had never seen men fight more bravely than those who boarded the *Hope* that day. There is therefore ample reason to devote some space to a

59

sketch of the principal *fidalgos* who crossed swords with
King James' men in the Persian Gulf three hundred
years ago.

First and foremost amongst these, was the man
selected to command the expedition fitted out at
Lisbon in the spring of 1619—Ruy Freyre d'Andrade.
Researches by the late Mr. W. Irvine, and by my
friend Snr. Frazão de Vasconcellos, have shown that
Ruy Freyre was born in the town of Beja in Alentejo.
He was the son of João Freyre d'Andrade, who was
Chancellor of India during the first decade of the
seventeenth century, and thus the holder of the
highest law office of the Crown. This João Freyre
was an intimate friend of the chronicler Diogo do
Couto, as may be seen from the correspondence
between them, printed on pp. 78-81 of Caminha's
Obras ineditas de Diogo do Couto, Lisboa, 1808. In
the Torre de Tombo there is a reference to the
grant of the captaincy of Damão to Ruy Freyre
d'Andrade as the eldest son of João Freyre. Ruy
Freyre first went out to India in 1607, in the fleet of
Dom Jeronimo Coutinho, as an ordinary *fidalgo*, or
private gentleman, with an allowance of 2,000 *reis* a
month. No portrait of him has survived, but he
stands clearly before us in the pages of Purchas, where
a servant of John Company, who knew him well,
describes him as being " a proper tall Gentleman,
swarthie of colour, sterne of Countenance, few of words
and of an excellent spirit ; he had lived here in India
many years." From 1609 onwards he spent every year
of his life on active service ; for the first eight or nine
years as Captain-Major of various Portuguese forces on
the North-west coast of India, defending the cities of
Chaul, Bassein and Damão against the assaults of
neighbouring princes ; and from 1619, until his death
thirteen years later, fighting the English and Persians

60

in the Gulf. The scholarly Della Valle, who came from Persia to India in one of the ships which had participated in the taking of Ormuz, testifies to the admiration in which he was held by his opponents, which not even his ruthless execution of the hapless survivors of the *Lion*, burnt by him off Gombrun in 1625, could altogether forfeit. The streak of cruelty in his character is also clearly brought out by the pitiless way with which he destroyed every living thing, regardless of age or sex, which fell into his hands during his campaigns in the Gulf. Of his headlong courage, open-handed generosity and somewhat capricious pride, several stories are told by Antonio Bocarro and other contemporary writers, from which we select the following.

During a sortie from Damão in 1613, Ruy Freyre slew a Pathan in single combat, cutting him clean in half at the waist with a single sweep of his sword. Whilst serving as Captain of Chaul in the following year, he was severely wounded by a musket shot in the stomach, during an attack upon a superior force of the enemy ; his troops on seeing this, fell into confusion, but Ruy Freyre, despite the gravity of his wound, rallied them by his voice and example, until a retirement was effected in good order. During these campaigns he kept open house for scores of the poorer soldiers, and raised and equipped a force of native auxiliaries at his own expense.[1] In November, 1615, he was appointed Captain-Major of the Bombay flotilla, which visited Surat on its voyage to Diu, in order to confirm the peace recently agreed upon with

[1]Bocarro, *Decada* 13 (Lisbon, 1876), pp. 71-73, 218-220 and 266-267. Faria y Sousa also reproduces these stories with less exactitude and detail in Vol. III of his *Asia Portuguesa*, (Lisboa, 1675). It is worth noting that at the time of his appointment to the command of the Persian Gulf squadron in 1619, Ruy Freyre was only 28 or 29 years old. His orders for the expedition are printed on pp. 211-218 of the *Commentaries*, (English edition).

the Moghul authorities. Ruy Freyre's fame had preceeded him, but the local Nabob had a still higher opinion of him, when he found that he refused to receive the customary bribes and gifts which all previous Portuguese officers had accepted without shame. Ruy Freyre was indeed eventually persuaded to accept a Kashmir shawl, but he then told his assembled captains that he was determined to present it to the one whose mistress was by common consent agreed to be the most beautiful—a certain Hippolyto Furtado being judged the lucky man after a deal of friendly rivalry.[1] On his return voyage to Goa with the same convoy in January, 1616, his flotilla was scattered by a storm, and two of the merchant vessels were captured by pirate craft who were lying in wait on the outskirts of the fleet. So indignant was Ruy Freyre that the vessels had not followed his poop-lantern, which he had kept burning all night despite the fury of the storm, that he shaved the beards of all the soldiers in their six consorts as a punishment. In view of these and many other similar exploits of his, it is not surprising that he was famed far and wide throughout the seaboard of Western India ; and when peace had been concluded in 1615, hundreds of Mahratta warriors flocked to Chaul to see him. Incidentally, Bocarro informs us that he was singularly successful as a trainer of native troops, and could organise the most unpromising material into well-trained and hard-fighting soldiers.

Whilst Ruy Freyre's expedition was being fitted out

---

[1]Bocarro, *Decada* 13, pp. 164-165. Danvers in his *Portuguese in India*, makes a muddle of this anecdote which is typical of his slipshod and superficial work. He states that the shawl was awarded by the verdict of the Captains to Hippolyto Furtado, who was mistress of Ruy Freyre. This error is all the more ludicrous, as we learn from Faria y Sousa, whence Danvers mistranslated his version, that Ruy Freyre was unusually chaste for a man of his age and race—never having had a consort of any kind. And yet people persist in quoting Danvers as a reliable authority.

in the Tagus, the English were having things their own way in the Persian Gulf. The first venture in the *James* in 1616, had been followed up by the despatch of the *Bee* from Surat in the following year, though she arrived practically empty. Amongst the factors on board her was Edward Monnox, who may be regarded as the real founder of the English position in the Gulf, and to whose entertaining pen we owe the best account of events in Persia during the next five years. Even before the agreement made by the first factor, Edward Connock, with Shah Abbas in August, 1617, had been signed, the English had not omitted to stir up the " Sophy " against the Portuguese. Fearful lest the Lusitanians might spoil the Company's promised monopoly of the Persian silk export trade, " the only richest yet known in the world," Connock had tried " with reasons unanswerable to persuade this Prince what society, honour, benefit he may attain in freeing his gulfs of their present slavery, by taking Ormuz into his possession, an act worthy himself, easily performed, and whereby he may be Lord of his own." The ease with which Ormuz might have been taken at this time, is likewise emphasized by Don Garcia de Silva in his *Commentarios*. This worthy, who had been delayed in Goa for nearly two years, owing to the procrastination of the jealous Portuguese authorities, had at length reached Ormuz in April 1617, only to find the place in a lamentable condition. So struck was he with the apparent defencelessness of the town, that he renounced his former decision of not proceeding on his embassy until the Shah had restored Bahrein, Gombrun and Kishm to the titular King of Ormuz, and resolved to continue his mission forthwith, if only to spin out the negotiations in order to gain time to put the place into a state of defence. He crossed over to the mainland in October, but despite

63

the fact that his fruitless mission lasted two years, he found Ormuz still utterly unprepared to stand a siege, on his return from the Shah's court in October, 1619. Insult was added to injury by the fact that he was compelled to kick his heels in Ormuz during the winter months, as the reported presence of an English fleet at Jask, was sufficient to scare the Portuguese to such an extent that they dared not send any ships to Goa before April, 1620. He tried to utilise his forced sojourn in the town, by inducing the captain Dom Luis de Souza to put the place in a state of defence, but could get no more backing from him than from his predecessor, Dom Luiz da Gama, whom he accused of intercepting his correspondence during his mission in Persia. To some of those not on the spot, the conquest of Ormuz did not appear quite so easy. Sir Thomas Roe, writing from India to William Robbins (Sir Robert Sherley's agent at Ispahan) in August, 1617, roundly scoffs at the idea that " we will take Ormuz and beat the Portugal out of those seas ; these are but vanities." In other letters he repeated this warning, and frankly urged that the best service he could do the Company, would be to make peace with the Portuguese. Nevertheless he added that the " Portugals " were not wise enough to know their own weakness, and admitted that the Persian trade once begun, " though imperfectly," should not now be given over. He was however, almost alone in this opinion, and the men on the spot like Connock, Barker and Monnox were all confident of success.

The poor lading brought by the *Bee* in 1617, had been atoned for by the arrival of the *Expedition* at Jask in 1618 with two Portuguese prizes, " which are very useful for your occaisions," worth some £2,000 or £3,000. The Shah, who had by now finally, if secretly, resolved to break with the Portuguese, showed himself especially gracious towards the English in the following year; for he received some letters sent by King James from the hands of the English factors, at a "princely and sumptuous banquet, whereto he invited all foreign ambassadors resident in his Court, viz., the Spanish, Indian, Turkish, Russian, Tartarian and Uzbeck" emissaries. " Glorying no doubt," the factors added complacently, " to have it published in an assembly of so many repugnant and discrepant nations, that it hath pleased so potent and yet so far remote and diffident a prince to direct his royal letters to him." Under the influence of wine the "Sophy's" benevolence went even further, and he whispered to the factors " that he had a resolution to take Ormuz from the King of Spain and deliver it unto the English nation; " though they later complained of his " fair promises but contrary performances." Shah Abbas, on his side, had some complaints to make about the inadequacy of the English shipping and their cargoes, which caused the factors to press for a fleet to be sent, the more so since there was always the chance of a single vessel being intercepted by the Portuguese, weak as they were.[1]

The preparation of Ruy Freyre's expedition in the Tagus had not escaped the notice of the East India Company, who duly warned their representatives at Surat of its intended despatch and destination. Consequently, it was decided to send the whole of the squadron of three ships which came out from England in the autumn of 1619, together with the ship *Lion*, to Jask, whither they set sail in November, returning to Surat again in the middle of the following January, without having seen anything of the expected Portuguese armada. The mere appearance of Bickley's

[1]*Calendar of State Papers, East Indies*, 1617-1621, pp. 303-311.

squadron threw the Portuguese at Ormuz into a shameful panic, which Don Garcia de Silva did his best to allay, but without much success. His description of the consternation caused by the news of the presence of the English ships at Jask, is confirmed by Monnox who jubilantly reported : " As we increase so doth Ormuz decrease ; for the very report of the arrival of five English ships in Jask did strike such terror and amazement into these hen-hearted inhabitants, that even their own houses and churches escaped not the fury of their mattocks and pick-axes, fearing lest the English in landing should possess themselves of the said churches and houses, and therein lay siege and battery into their invincible fort."[1]

From this panic mood the Portuguese were delivered by the arrival of the long-expected squadron of Ruy Freyre at Ormuz in June, 1620, after a disastrous voyage, during which one vessel had been lost off Melinde, whilst the remainder of the squadron had wintered at Mozambique where many of the crew died. Further time was lost in cruising off the entrance to the Red Sea, for Indian or Arab vessels unprovided with Portuguese passes ; and the condition of the survivors on reaching Ormuz was such as to justify the English sneer that they were only " fightable till they fly." Nevertheless the factors at Jask reported that with the arrival of Ruy Freyre's squadron, " the Portugals are grown great men, and begin to look big," and it speedily became apparent that the English would not be able to fetch their silks away this year without a struggle.[2]

[1]*Idem*, p. 353. *L'Ambassade de D. Garcias de Silva Figeroa en Perse*, (Paris, 1667), pp. 371-391.

[2]*Cal. S.P. East Indies*, 1617-1621, p. 379. The outward voyage of Ruy Freyre's fleet is described in full in Chapters I to III of the *Commentaries of Ruy Freyre d'Andrade*, (London, 1929). *Cf* also Foster, *English Factories in India*, 1619-1621, pp. xxvii-xxix.

On arriving at Ormuz, Ruy Freyre made several additions and alterations to his fleet, and then sailed to Jask in November, 1620, with the intention of intercepting the English ships expected to arrive there in December, to fetch the 520 bales of silk contracted for by Monnox. His force comprised the galleons *São Pedro* (64) which served as flagship ; *São Martinho* (48) second-in-command ; the *pataxo*, or pinnace, *São Lourenço* (24) and the *urca*, or hulk, *Nossa Senhora da Conceição* (22), these two last vessels being Flemish-built ships. In addition, there were a number of galliots and other oared craft to serve as despatch boats and scouts, whilst the whole Armada was manned by over 1,000 men, the majority of them soldiers, for the European sailors and gunners were few and far between. With this fleet the Captain-Major took up his appointed station off Jask.

Ruy Freyre had been at sea for exactly a month, when two English vessels hove in sight on the 16th December, with a Portuguese prize they had taken on the voyage. These were the *Hart* and *Eagle*, which Captain Andrew Shilling, commander of this year's outward-bound fleet, had detached from his squadron in accordance with the Company's instructions, a few days before reaching Swalley Hole with his two remaining vessels, the *London* and *Roebuck*. The Portuguese at once weighed to attack the English, who thinking themselves no match for the four galleons, abandoned their prize and put about for Surat under cover of darkness.[1] Meanwhile Shilling had arrived

---

[1] The anonymous author of the *True Relation of that worthy sea-fight*, etc., is not very complimentary about the behaviour of the *Hart* and *Eagle*, alleging : " But the truth is, they were very rich themselves, and loath to lose all by any misadventure, which they might escape, and not wilfully run into ; and yet I must confesse, they had many motives to fight with them, and daring hearts to the encounter ; [yet] for all their great burthen and preparation, well, they did not . . . "

at Swalley with his other two ships, but the Surat factors, knowing of the peril to which the *Hart* and *Eagle* were exposed owing to the presence of Ruy Freyre's squadron off Jask, hurried him off again to the support of his consorts, " for they knewe, they should bee fought with all, if not over-set." Some of his captains were not too keen to go, although they realised " it was not our turnes to dispute, nor had we any other part to play but obedience, and so wee put to sea againe, taking a course to follow our shipps." The *London* and *Roebuck* had not been two days on their voyage when they captured a Portuguese vessel from Muscat laden with raisins, dates and forty-two Arabian horses,[1] whilst shortly after this event, they fell in with the *Hart* and *Eagle*. The crews of these latter vessels gave an account of their flight from Ruy Freyre's squadron, " whose strength and preparation they reported extraordinary . . . discoursing at large of the matter, and describing the manner of the enemies watches, and how bravely and warlike they were appointed." Shilling however, was not the man to be daunted by any display of force, and he resolved to take in his lading at Jask roads, even if he had to try a bout with the redoubtable Ruy Freyre, " whom themselves call the Pride of Portugal." The united squadron accordingly headed for Jask, the prize having been prepared for use as a fireship if necessary. Shilling's determined character is well shown from the fact that when some people demurred at this step, " as pittying the loss of so many brave horses, he as bravely replied, how doe they doe then in the wars, when they are compelled to kill their prisoners in colde blood ; and therefore think neither of scruple, or nicety, but let us follow the businesse we take in hand."

[1] The *Nossa Senhora das Merces*, of 200 tons, Captain Francisco Miranda.

The rival squadrons came in sight of each other at sunset on Christmas day, but battle was not joined until the following morning, when Ruy Freyre's galleons came out of the road, " and in a daring and braving manner invited us to an encounter, which we intertained with many Navall ceremonies, and putting out our collours of defiance, with the adorning our ships to answere their proportion of Gallantnesse, we made a brave show, as if we meant to intertaine death and slaughter with mirth and jollitie." In this manner they approached, until the *São Pedro* and *London* lay less than a musket shot apart, when Ruy Freyre, who was standing on the half-deck of his flagship dressed in rose-coloured camlet, took a goblet of wine from an attendant page and drank Shilling's health, to which the Englishman replied in a similar fashion. As a gesture of mutual defiance, the two leaders then hurled their goblets into the sea, whilst to the sound of drum and trumpet, both sides fell to it with a will.

The ensuing fight has been described elsewhere, so need only be briefly recorded here.[1] The action raged until the exhausted combatants were parted by nightfall, but the advantage lay chiefly with the English. They had, it is true, prematurely fired their prize " when there was neither reason nor cause . . . and leaving us in a kind of confusion to see so many goodly horses perish in the raging Sea," but the slaughter caused by the English cannon on board the overcrowded Portuguese galleons was appalling. On

[1] The best account from the English side is that of Richard Swan, master of *The Roebuck*, printed on pp. 220-225, of the 1618-1621 volume of Foster's *English Factories in India*, q.v., for other versions. Another valuable source is the excessively rare little tract, *The true Relation of that worthy sea-fight*, (London, 1622), whence most of the quotations in the text are taken. Unfortunately no trustworthy Portuguese account has come down to us, the only ones available being translated in my edition of the *Commentaries of Ruy Freyre d'Andrade*, (London, 1929), pp. xxv-xxvii, 21-30 and 298-301.

the next day the wind was in favour of the Portuguese, but they made no attempt to interfere with the English, who stood into Jask roads and landed their goods. Ruy Freyre remained in the offing, and on New Year's day, 1621 he received a supply of men and munitions which had been sent him in some small craft from Ormuz. Thus reinforced, he accepted a renewed challenge of the English on January 7th. This action ended even more disastrously for the Portuguese than the former, partly owing to the greatly superior gunnery of the English, and partly to the mistaken tactics adopted by Ruy Freyre, who insisted on fighting with his ships moored in a line, against the advice of his most experienced officers, who were in favour of getting under sail. As a result of this foolish decision, one of the galleons, whose cable had been cut by a cannon ball, drifted athwart of the two vessels moored in rear of her, so that (it being flat calm at the time), all these ships remained board on board of each other, and exposed to the full effect of the raking English broadsides, without being able to use more than two or three of their own guns. The Portuguese endured this terrible punishment for some hours, until finally at three o'clock in the afternoon, " unwilling after so hotte a dinner to receive the like supper, they cutte their cables and drove with the tide (then setting westerly) untill they were without reach of our gunnes ; and then their frigattes came to them and towed them awaie wonderfullie mangled and torne." The English were not further molested, and were enabled to lade the silk and depart for Surat at their leisure.[1]

[1] The casualties in these actions were amazingly disproportionate, even making due allowance for the poor gunnery of the Portuguese. The total English losses did not exceed ten, though they included Captain Shilling, who was mortally wounded during the second day's fight. The Portuguese confessed to a casualty list of over 430, which is hardly surprising, in view of the fact that Richard Swan states the four English vessels expended a total of 4,021 " great shot," most of them at short range, during the two battles.

Whilst this campaign was in progress, the aged Governor of India, Fernão de Albuquerque, had been doing his best to assemble further reinforcements at Goa for Ruy Freyre's squadron. Despite the chronic state of penury and want of European sailors, with which the Portuguese authorities invariably had to struggle, he had succeeded in fitting out two strongly-built galleons,[1] manned with 270 men, by the end of the year 1620 ; but did not venture to despatch them, for fear lest they should fall into the hands of Shilling's squadron, which he knew was on the way to Jask. With the return of the English ships to Swally in February 1621, the coast was clear, and the galleons left for Ormuz on the 6th April, carrying a large supply of munitions in addition to their crews. By these ships, the Governor wrote letters to Ruy Freyre, impressing upon him the necessity for preparing his armada, thus reinforced, for another struggle with the English off Jask in the coming winter. These appeals fell on deaf ears, for Ruy Freyre had decided to carry out the second part of the commission with which he had been sent out from Lisbon, namely to build a fort in the neighbouring island of Kishm (Qishm). The object of this plan was to gain control of some wells situated at the eastern extremity of this island and thereby secure compensation for the loss of the wells at Gombrun, taken by the Persians some

[1] *Todolos Santos* and *Nossa Senhora da Victoria*. The former was a very famous ship which had served as the flagship of Don Hieronymo de Azevedo in his fruitless attack on Downton's squadron at Swally Hole in 1615. The Governor admitted that the quality of their crews was very poor, owing to the fact that the news of Ruy Freyre's ill success at Jask had disheartened the men ; hence he had been forced to embark many convicted criminals, whom he had taken from the jails, or induced to return from the dominions of neighbouring native princes, by a public proclamation of free pardon for all offences save sodomy, counterfeiting coinage and heresy. See the interesting letters written by Fernão de Albuquerque to Ruy Freyre in March, 1621, as printed on pp. 186-191 of Luciano Cordeiro's *Como se perdeu Ormuz*.

six years previously. This move was not only ill-timed, but unnecessary; for as long as the Portuguese maintained their command of the sea in the Persian Gulf, they could land on Kishm and draw water from its wells at any time they liked; whilst conversely, if the mastery was allowed to pass to the English, then they would not have access to the wells at Kishm or anywhere else. These considerations, and others equally potent, were urged upon Ruy Freyre by Fernão d'Albuquerque and by the Captain of Ormuz, Dom Francisco de Sousa, both of whom clearly saw that all depended upon retaining command of the sea by defeating the English off Jask. The hot-headed Ruy Freyre however, either would not listen to reason, or else despaired of defeating the English at sea; and gained his own way by producing at a full council meeting held in Ormuz Castle, the Royal orders for the speedy erection of a fort at Kishm.

Accordingly on 7th May, 1621, Ruy Freyre left Ormuz for Kishm at the head of an expeditionary corps of some 2,000 seasoned Portuguese soldiers and 1,000 Arab auxiliaries, embarked in a fleet of 33 sail, which likewise carried the frame of the proposed fort. A landing was effected the next day, in the face of an obstinate resistance by the Persian troops, and Ruy Freyre at once set about the construction of the fort. This was built " of a great height and thicknesse, with halfe-moones and flanckers very artificially, which in five moneths and a halfe hee had finished; a thing wonderfull in so short a time to be effected," as a contemporary Englishman described it. The Persian forces in the island were speedily reinforced by levies from the mainland under the command of Imam Quli Khan who directed the operations as Governor of Fars. The Persians closely besieged the fortress for nine months, but all their efforts to take it proved vain;

whilst Ruy Freyre carried the war into the enemy's camp, by means of plundering flotillas of light craft which he sent out to ravage the neighbouring coasts and islands. No quarter was given by the Portuguese during these destructive raids on the costal towns and villages, but they did not serve to effect much more than heighten the hatred of the Persians for their savage opponents.

So long as Ruy Freyre held command of the sea, it was clear to all concerned that the Persians could never capture Kishm fort, much less Ormuz, and it did not take the Persian authorities long to make up their minds to secure the active assistance of the English, at all costs. Both sides knew that the annual English squadron to fetch the silks, would be due off Jask in November or December as usual. Both Fernão de Albuquerque and Dom Francisco de Sousa had urged upon Ruy Freyre the importance of waylaying the English off this port in order to prevent at any price their effecting a junction with the Persian army.[1] Ruy Freyre however considered that his duty lay in Kishm fort, which he refused to abandon, and the most he would consent to do, was to agree to proceed to Ormuz to take command of the galleons, on a signal gun being fired from the castle, when and

[1]When Fernão de Albuquerque heard that Ruy Freyre had constructed the fort in Kishm, against his repeated advice, with the result that he was closely besieged by an overwhelming Persian force, he wrote him a letter in which the following interesting lines occur : " it had been just and right if you had considered my previous warnings, and not been so confident of yourself, before putting hand to that work ; for you with your thirty years had not been dreamt of in this world, when I was already old in years of experience and his Majesty's service in these parts ; and yet they tell me that you were fully persuaded you could correct what my seventy years wrote you, in so weighty and important a matter . . ." In this letter, the Governor also urged on Ruy Freyre the advisability of proceeding to the Coromandel coast after refitting his squadron, as he had news of three ill-manned and newly arrived Danish vessels off that coast, which would be an easy prey. He also suggested that Ruy Freyre could refit in Goa if necessary, after which he could seek out the English off Swally, or Tiwai, near Muscat. (Letter of Fernão de Albuquerque 21/x/1621.)

if the English fleet should appear. This voluntary abandonment of the offensive to the enemy met with its due retribution. A strong squadron of nine ships under the command of Captains Blyth and Weddell reached Jask on Christmas Eve 1621, and the Khan of Shiras at once applied to the commanders for their assistance against the Portuguese, threatening to prohibit them from trading at all, in the event of their not complying with his request. The English captains urged on by Monnox, were nothing loath to fall in with his plans and, despite some " murmuring among the commonality," they induced their crews to follow them. An agreement was speedily concluded with the Khan of Shiras for the conduct of combined operations against the Portuguese by land and sea, on the general basis of (1) the castle of Ormuz to be handed over to the English on its capture ; (2) the spoil to be equally divided between Persians and English ; (3) the English to be for ever Customs-free ; (4) the Christian captives to be at the disposal of the English and the Moslems at that of the Persians, whilst (5) the latter would pay half the cost of the upkeep of the English fleet during the operations.[1] This treaty was concluded at Kuhistak, whither the English had gone from Jask, as being a better port and nearer the scene of action, on the 5th January, 1622 ; and at the end of the month, having embarked the silks lest the Persians should play them false, the English squadron stood over to Ormuz.

Weddell and Blyth hoped that the galleons moored under the Castle would come out and fight them, but nothing of the sort occurred. Some Portuguese accounts allege that the agreed signal for the recall of

---

[1]This is the gist of the agreement as stated by Monnox. Other contemporary copies (i.e., that in *Records relating to Persia*, Vol. I), state that the Castle was to be garrisoned equally by Persians and English, with a Governor for each.

Ruy Freyre from Kishm, was made from the Castle, but that it passed unnoticed in the besieged fort. Be that as it may, neither the acting admiral of the fleet, Luis de Brito, nor the newly elected Captain of the fortress, Simão de Mello Pereira, had any stomach for the fight, and they made no move.[1] The English, understanding that Ruy Freyre was at Kishm, did not waste any further time, but sailed across to this island, where they arrived on February 2nd, " in fit time to save both the lives and reputations of the Portugals, not able long to hold out against the Persian siege, and willing rather to yield to us." At first the Portuguese " weived us with naked swords ; yet one more wiser than the rest, hunge out a napkin or white cloth, whereupone in Christianlike compassion, Edward Monnox was sent on shoare to parlie with them." He was duly admitted to the presence of Ruy Freyre, " And beinge sett together in the courte of guard, the sayd Rufrero began with a long storye of the antient love and amytie betwene the two nations, English and Portugalls, and the noble acts that the English had done in asistinge the Portugalls to expulse the Moors out of their countrye ;[2] to which the said Monox

[1] Luis de Brito, a cousin of Fernão de Albuquerque, had gone to Ormuz in the galleon *Todolos Santos* in April, 1621, whilst Simão de Mello, who had gone as commander of a flotilla in November of the same year, succeeded to the captaincy of Ormuz Castle on the death of Dom Francisco de Sousa. He had previously served as Captain of Mombasa and of the Malabar fleet. After the fall of Ormuz, Simão de Mello fled to the domains of the Adil Shah, Raja of Bijapur, whence he subsequently proceeded to the Coromandel coast near São Thomé. Here he led a fugitive existence as a kind of hermit, but he remained in touch with the authorities at Goa, acting as a sort of spy on their behalf. An interesting letter of his to the Conde de Linhares, is printed in the latter's *Diario*. Amongst other things, de Mello discusses a project for the capture of the Danish Fortress of Tranquebar. Luis de Brito was more unlucky, being apprehended by the authorities and executed at Goa in 1622.

[2] This is of course a reference to the English crusaders who assisted Dom Affonso Henriques, the founder of the Portuguese monarchy to wrest Lisbon from the Moors in 1147. (*Cf.* Professor Gibb's lecture on *English Crusaders*

replyed hee came not to treate of busynisses of such antequitye, but hee came to treate of sattisfaxione and revenge for the warre begun and attempted by himselfe, the their present Rufrero, against our last yeares fleete in the Roade of Jasques, to the losse of our worthy commander and our King's sworne servante, besydes other of His Majistis subjects." Ruy Freyre retorted that he had only acted in accordance with his orders, but after much dispute he seemed disposed to surrender on terms to the English. He demanded however, that the same conditions should be extended to his Arab auxiliaries, of whom there were some two hundred in the fort; but Monnox told him that these would have to be handed over to the Khan of Shiras, in accordance with the terms of the Anglo-Persian agreement. "Then sayd Rufrero: 'Rather than wee will doe that, wee will ende our lives together'" and so vehemently did he say this, that Monnox promised to intercede on their behalf with Imam Quli Khan. He did in fact obtain from the Persian General a verbal promise that their lives should be spared, but Ruy Freyre absolutely refused to accept this, and broke off all further negotiations. The English thereupon bombarded the fort, which they soon reduced to a sorry plight. Ruy Freyre now called on the garrison to sally forth and end their lives fighting to the last;

---

in Portugal.) On the first appearance of the English fleet off Kishm, Ruy Freyre had also sent the commanders a letter couched in the same strain. After recalling the exploits of the English crusaders and of John of Gaunt in the Peninsula, (*Cf.* Mr. C. H. Williams' lecture on this last subject) he asked them to refrain from helping the Persians "so that wee may reserve our dissentions for other voyages, in which by valourous contending may be satisfied those wrongs that cannot well be remembered in such times as these are," and concluded defiantly by declaring that in the event of the English persisting in their intentions, "the first wee hope for is no more than to provide ourselves to die, defending that with Arms, wee have gotten by Arms." (Ruy Freyre to the commanders of the English fleet, 1/ii/1622; contemporary translation in Monnox's *History at large of the taking of Ormuz Castle*; India Office, *Original Correspondence*, 1032).

but some friars dissuaded the men from following him and induced them to reopen negotiations with the English, after disarming their leader and imprisoning him in his quarters. An agreement was speedily concluded, whereby the Portuguese garrison was allowed to proceed to Ormuz after having been disarmed ; whilst the hapless Arab auxiliaries were handed over to the tender mercies of the Persians, " who formerly had promysed them mercie, but falsely murthered them most unhumanly." Ruy Freyre himself was delivered by his men to the English who shipped him on board the *Lion*, together with some of his captains, as prisoners to Surat.[1]

Ruy Freyre was well treated by his captors who admired him unreservedly, which was hardly the case with some of his own countrymen. How these regarded his conduct at Kishm, is well shown by the following extracts from a letter written by the Archbishop of Goa, Dom Frei Christovão de Lisboa, to Fernão de Albuquerque on hearing of the loss of the fort. " Your Worship should not despair nor become angered at the affair of Kishm, because it could have come to no other end, since that fortress was founded at such an unseasonable time, as we always said ; whilst their Lordships of the Council in Madrid ever expected more of it, than we here from our own experience and knowledge. Neither do I blame the soldiers in what they did, according to what I have heard from Brother Mezanha ; for what Ruy Freyre wished to do, was rather the deed of a barbarian than of a Christian, and the courage of despair rather than that of strength ; for every day we see positions evacuated and armies in

[1]The best English account of the siege and fall of Kishm fort is contained in the documents calendared on pp. 31-38 of Foster's *English Factories in India*, 1622-1623, whence most of the above quotations are taken. The only lengthy Portuguese account extant is that given in Chapters 24-29 of the *Commentarios*, but this is a bombastic and unreliable version in the main.

retreat without shame, and it was more prudent to make terms with the English than for so many soldiers barbarously to die in vain ; as it is certain that ten soldiers are worth more to us, than ten thousand to the Shah, and even so, the affair was ended better than I had expected . . . the Fortress [of Ormuz] is safe and your Worship should send a good Captain for the fleet ; there is no need to worry about the possibility of recapturing Kishm, now or ever, because, so long as we have control of the sea, they can never stop us watering in so large an island, whilst if we have not command of the sea, events have shown that the place will always be more of a hindrance than a help. And even though your Worship should realise all these things perfectly, yet I could not forbear informing you that I was of your opinion, as I always have been in this matter ; and that the blame of everything lies on Ruy Freyre, who impoverished the state for the glory of making a fortress, and who abandoned his armada for the sake of defending it. His Majesty should trust more in us who are on the spot, and not so much in the ministers at Madrid, who cannot know as much of these regions as we."[1]

A few days after the surrender of Kishm and the joint occupation of its fortress by an Anglo-Persian detachment, the English squadron sailed to Gombrun, where the officers and men were royally feasted by the grateful Khan of Shiras, who was nevertheless chagrined that the English would not surrender Ruy Freyre to him. The withdrawal of the fleet to Gombrun had

---

[1]Document printed on pp. 197-198 of *Como se perdeu Ormuz*. This statement supports the version narrated in the *Commentaries*, and provides a satisfactory refutation of the hints thrown out by D. Garcia da Silva y Figeroa in his journal, that Ruy Freyre did not oppose the surrender of the fort. Incidentally, the Archbishop's letter affords yet another instance of the continual ill-feeling between the Spaniards and Portuguese at this date, and the mutual suspicion with which they regarded each other.

an unforeseen effect on the attitude of Simão de Mello, Captain of Ormuz, who wrote to the Governor of India that the English having accomplished their object and laden the silks, would return to Surat and leave Ormuz unmolested. He added that if they should come after all, he was confident that he could prevent either Persians or English from setting foot in the island.[1] This arrogant boast was soon put to the test, for on Saturday, February 19th, six English vessels hove in sight accompanied by an enormous flotilla of small craft carrying some 3,000 Persian soldiery, and the whole force anchored at a distance of about six miles from the Castle at sunset. Next day, the Persians under the command of Imam Quli Khan landed without opposition, and marched with a great show of resolution on the city. Simão de Mello, for all his previous bragging and sneers at Ruy Freyre, had completely lost his head on the appearance of the Anglo-Persian armada and had made no attempt to resist the disembarkation, as he might easily have done.[2] A few men had been posted behind barricades erected in the *Maidan* or market square, " but the Persians soone made way, and the Portugalls like so many sheepe tooke their heels into their Castle." Two valiant captains, Dom Gonçalo da Silveira and Luis de Moura Rolim, attempted to stay the panic, but their efforts were without avail and in this manner the Persians occupied and sacked the city.

[1]Letter of Simão de Mello for Fernão de Albuquerque, 7/ii/1622 (*Como se perdeu Ormuz*, p. 199-200). Three of the English ships, including the *Lion* with Ruy Freyre on board, were sent back to Surat at this time, which may have had the effect of confirming Simão de Mello in his erroneous opinion.

[2]Simão de Mello's own excuse for the lack of resistance offered, was that the majority of the soldiers available were unarmed, having just come from Kishm, where they had been deprived of their weapons by the English on evacuating the fort.

There are several detailed and reliable accounts of the siege of Ormuz Castle available in print, and it is therefore not necessary to give here more than the briefest outline of the progress of the siege.[1] The English devoted their efforts principally to destroying the galleons moored close under the castle walls ; and in this they were so successful, that by the first week in April they had sunk or burnt them all, including the flagship *São Pedro*, which after being set on fire by a daring cutting-out expedition one night, drifted, a blazing wreck, over to the shore near Gombrun where she sank. Meanwhile they had landed from the ships some heavy guns which kept up a practically continuous bombardment of the Castle, under cover of which the Persians dug their approach trenches as far as the foot of the bastion of *Santiago*. They next resorted to mining, and though the Portuguese endeavoured to forestall them by counter-mining, a part of the bastion was blown up on March 27th, causing a breach, through which although " it proved somewhat difficulte and bad to enter, yet the Persians gave a very resolute assault thereunto, but it was so well defended by the Portugalls, that the Persians were forced for that time to retire." Monnox sharply criticised the lack of discipline which prevailed amongst the Persians, to which he attributed

---

[1] The fullest account on the English side is Monnox's *History at large of the taking of Ormuz Castle*, printed in part by Purchas in Vol. II of the 1625 edition of his *Pilgrimes* and first printed in full from the original manuscript in the India Office as an Appendix to the English edition of the *Commentaries of Ruy Freyre d'Andrade*. Other valuable contemporary sources will be found mentioned in this work, and in the 1622-1623 volume of Foster's *English Factories in India* series. Herbert, Della Valle and others give hearsay and less reliable narratives. On the Portuguese side, the longest account is to be found in Chapters 30-41 of the *Commentaries of Ruy Freyre d'Andrade*, whilst the relations of Simão de Mello, Manuel Borges de Sousa and other participants, which are printed in the appendices to this work, will also be found useful, and in places more reliable. Another valuable source is the depositions of many witnesses of the siege printed on pp. 205-293 of *Como se perdeu Ormuz*. Both English and Portuguese versions agree well enough together, when due allowance is made for their different standpoints.

most of their ill-success, " for as the old proverb is they entred without fear or witt, for when the Portugale came to the push of the pike with them, they had never a pike to answer them, and soe with shame were constrained to give back, and lost that with dishonour which they might have maintained with credit."

The Persian army was singularly ill-equipped for a siege, being poorly supplied with powder and shot ; but the former being liberally provided by the English, they continued their sapping and mining of the *Santiago* bastion to such good effect that they were enabled to make a second assault on the 27th April. This attack was carried out by a force of at least two thousand men " who very resolutely ranne up the breach into a part of the Bulwarke which they might wholly have possessed that very instant, had they not at first made such haste as to runne their resolution out of breath ; insomuch that onely eight or ten Portugals and a few Negros, made them onely with their Rapiers to give ground and to retire themselves unto the very outward skirt of the Bulwarke, where they had not roome for fortie men to stand in the face of their Enemie, yet there they barricaded themselves. Which before they could affect to their purpose, the Portugall plyed two or three pieces of ordnance from one of his Flankers that lay open unto them, in such sort, that they sent some scores of them to carry newes unto their Prophet Mortus Ali, that more of his Disciples would shortly be with him." Despite the heavy losses suffered by the Persians from the raking fire of the Portuguese guns, and from the hand-grenades and powder-pots which the " Portugals bestowed as liberally as if they had come from the mouth of Hell," the attackers hung on to the lodgement thus effected in the *Santiago* bastion. In the course of three days' furious hand to hand fighting, the

Persians gradually extended their hold over the whole bulwark and could not be dislodged by the gallant counter-attacks of the defenders led by the heroic Dom Gonçalo da Silveira in person.

By the end of April, the situation of the besieged was critical in the extreme. The bastion of *Santiago* was held by the enemy, who could overlook part of the Castle therefrom, whilst other mines had been sprung, or dug, beneath the bastion of *São Pedro*, the Cavalier bulwark and the Cistern. Provisions were running short, being limited to some rice and salted fish, " two very good preparatives to a cup of good drinke if they had it," as Monnox sarcastically observed ; dysentry and enteric fever raged amongst the hundreds cooped up in the cramped space within the Castle walls, where the bodies of the slain lay about unburied with " cats and dogs eating them, with infinite many flies." Many of the Castle's canon had been damaged or dismounted, whilst most of the best soldiers were either killed or wounded, and the survivors almost exhausted by the strain of continual toil and fighting. The last hope of escape had gone when the galleons had been sunk or fired, and the prospect of help arriving from Goa seemed remote in the extreme. All things considered, it is not surprising that at this juncture the majority of the garrison mutinied and demanded that the Governor should come to terms with the English ; for all knew that there was no reason to expect mercy from the victorious Persians, although half-hearted negotiations had been going on with the latter, at intervals since April 6th. But there were still some dauntless spirits, who advocated that rather than surrender they should " put their Women and children with all their treasure into a house, and blow them all up with gunpowder (that the Turks should neither injoy their wealth nor abuse their Wives) which done, they would thrust themselves pell-mell with the Persians, and so end their dayes." Chief amongst these dauntless spirits was the indomitable Dom Gonçalo da Silveira, who, despite the fact that he was almost *hors de combat* from the numerous and severe wounds he had received whilst defending the breaches in the *Santiago* bastion, offered his assistance to the Governor in quelling the mutiny. Simão de Mello himself, however, if not secretly privy to the insubordination of his men, at any rate connived at it ; and rejecting Dom Gonçalo's offer, he permitted his second-in-command, Luis de Brito, to open negotiations with the English, on the basis of the surrender of the Castle to them, in exchange for a guarantee that its inmates would be shipped to Sohar and Muscat. The English were nothing loath to accept these terms, and after a brief discussion the Castle was surrendered to the Anglo-Persian commanders on the 3rd May, which, appropriately enough, coincided with St. George's day in the Gregorian calendar then used by the English.

We have seen (page 79) that when Weddell's ships returned after the capture of Kishm in February, three of the vessels had been detached and sent back to India, with the principal Portuguese prisoners taken. Amongst these was Ruy Freyre in the *Lion*, who was particularly well treated by his admiring captors, from the master, James Beversham, down to Thomas Winterbourne, the ship's cook, who never tired of making tasty dishes for the illustrious captive. The English had determined to hold Ruy Freyre as prisoner until they could secure the release of some of the crew of the *Unicorn*, who had been prisoners at Macau since the loss of their ship on the South China coast in 1619. Together with Ruy Freyre they had also captured his commission from the King of Spain, authorising him to attack English shipping in the Persian Gulf ; and this was of great importance to them, since it went a long way to justify their open hostilities against the Portuguese forts at Kishm and Ormuz, at a time when there was peace between England and Spain in Europe. They consequently kept a strict watch on their prisoner, but eventually Ruy Freyre succeeded in eluding them by means of the following trick.

On the pretext of celebrating Easter day, whilst the *Lion* was anchored with some other vessels in Swally roads, he obtained leave from his guardians to send for some wine from the neighbouring Portuguese settlement at Damão to celebrate the event. He was able to arrange for some of this wine to be drugged, and by inducing the ship's company to partake freely thereof, they were speedily reduced to a state of coma. Seizing his opportunity, Ruy Freyre (with three companions) lowered himself by a rope into the skiff which was moored astern, and made for the shore. His absence was speedily discovered and a hue and cry raised, but although the Governor of Surat sent out some cavalry to aid the English in scouring the countryside, the fugitives escaped with the loss of one of their number, who was drowned whilst the party were swimming across the Tapti River. By ten o'clock next morning Ruy Freyre was safe within the walls of Damão, whence he proceeded as speedily as possible with two small vessels to Muscat, with the object of running the blockade of Ormuz in order to assume command of the beleaguered fortress.[1]

[1]This is the version given in Chapter 42 of the *Commentaries* and it is supported to some extent by a letter written by Ruy Freyre from Damão to the President at Surat, acknowledging that he had made his escape owing to the drunkenness of the watch, and pledging his honour to secure the return of the *Unicorn's* captives. Most contemporary English and Dutch accounts agree in ascribing his escape to the negligence of the watch in leaving the

At Muscat he was joined by Constantino de Sá, who had been despatched to the relief of Ormuz on the 2nd April by the Governor, Fernão de Albuquerque, after he had received news at Goa of the loss of Kishm and siege of Ormuz. The united force of de Sá and Ruy Freyre, only amounted to some fifteen galliots and similar light craft, all of which together would not have been a match for any one of the English ships, with which flotilla they left Muscat early in May. They had not been more than one day at sea, when they fell in with some ships from Ormuz carrying the remnants of the garrison to safety, in accordance with the terms of the capitulation. On learning of the fall of the fortress, Ruy Freyre was all for pushing on with the utmost speed, for he pointed out that the English and Persians would probably be celebrating their success in drunken orgies, and that an unexpected attack by even so small a force as theirs, would have every chance of success.[1]

De Sá however was not made of such stern stuff as Ruy Freyre, and his heart had never been in the business at all, as was proved by the dilatory way in which he had brought his squadron from Goa. Glad

---

skiff moored astern of the ship, and say nothing about the drugged wine. Beversham was severely taken to task by the directors of the Company, on his return to England, and their annoyance was increased by the loss of Ruy Freyre's commission, which would have been a trump card in their hands against any complaint by the Spanish Ambassador. They also suspected that Beversham might have been bribed to let Ruy Freyre escape, as it was stated he had offered Weddell £1,000 to wink at it. Eventually however, Beversham seems to have cleared himself. (*Cal. S.P.E.I.*, 1622-1624, pp. 134, 136 and 252.) The date of Ruy Freyre's escape is variously given as the 26th March and 2nd April.

[1]This was certainly the case, to judge by Monnox's racy description of the confusion which prevailed in the city and castle during their pillage by the Anglo-Persian forces, a contest in which the Persians as the more numerous party easily bore away the palm. Needless to say, the Khan of Shiras had no intention of fulfilling the terms of his treaty with the English by allowing them any share in the government of the place, which remained a purely Persian garrison.

of the excuse to abandon the whole enterprise, which he had looked on from the beginning as doomed to failure, he paid no heed to the angry protests of Ruy Freyre, but, " like a dogg that has lost his tayle," put about and returned with his fleet to Muscat.

That Ruy Freyre's daring proposal to fall upon the English and Persians in the full flush of their success was a perfectly practicable one, is evident from the remarks made by Monnox in his Journal. All the time of the siege he had been worried by the lax discipline kept by both English and Persian commanders, and he was filled with anxiety at the thought of what would happen if a relieving squadron should unexpectedly appear from Goa. " I think," he wrote in his Journal on one occasion, " there is no man soe weake of understanding to thinke that the Vice Roy and other Portugall magistrates of Goa, will suffer soe famous a thing as is their Castle of Ormuz to be lost for want of succors, and wherein consisteth that succor but in sendinge a sufficient Armado to beate our Englishe shippes oute of their seas, which is not impossible to be don . . . we lull ourselves asleepe in securitie and cry Peace, Peace, before the warr is trulie begun. I feare before the Castle of Ormus be possest eyther by Persian or English, we shall singe a new songe, or els I will say we have bin more fortunate in the success than prudent in our proceedings ; but if it prove otherwise, the dishonour will be more to our selves and nation than some of us do dream off. I would that those whom it conserneth more nearly than it doth me, would leave looking after a little paultrie pillage in Ormus and looke to this busyness of greater consequence."[1] It was indeed fortunate for the

---

[1] Monnox's journal, under March 27th. It is interesting to note that Purchas has omitted this passage, as also many other similar outspoken criticisms, from his *précis* of the journal printed in Vol. II of the 1625 edition

English that Dom Constantino de Sá, and not Ruy Freyre, was in command of the flotilla which put back to Muscat in May, 1622.

Whilst these events were taking place in the Persian Gulf, the government at Madrid had neither been deaf to the appeals for assistance which reached them from Goa, nor blind to the fact that the victory of the English over Ruy Freyre's galleons would mean the end of the century-old Lusitanian predominance in Persian waters. In March, 1621, no fewer than eight sail were fitted out for the voyage to India, but of all these vessels, only one galleon, the *São João*, reached Goa in September, all of the others having lost their voyage. Indeed it seemed as if the very stars in their courses fought against the Portuguese, since of four other ships which left the Tagus a month later, not one succeeded in rounding the Cape of Good Hope.[1] On March 23rd, 1622, Sir Walter Aston, the English Ambassador at Madrid, reported that " about the

---

of his *Pilgrimes*. It may be added that some people at least obtained rather more than the " paultrie pillage " Monnox derides. Chief amongst the offenders was Woodcock, the master of the *Whale*, who was popularly believed to have acquired an immense store of ill-gotten wealth; the Spanish ambassador in England complained to King James I, " that the very dishes that the lowest and basest sort of the crew put their meat in are of silver, stamped with the arms of many families of Portugal, whom they have miserably sacked and slain." Despite these and other allegations, it is clear that the Company itself was a loser by the enterprise, from a financial point of view, whatever their servants on the spot might have secured for themselves.

[1]The carracks in question were *Nossa Senhora de Conceição*, *Santo Amaro* (which was wrecked at Mombassa); the galleons *Trindade*, *São Salvador*, *São Simão*, *Misericordia*, *Santo André* and *São João*. These were followed at the end of April by the *Santa Tereza*, *São Joseph*, *São Carlos* and *Santo Thomé*, who were likewise forced to return to Lisbon.

19th of this month, there departed from Lisbon four caracques with a new Vice-King for Goa, and in their company four tall ships of war with soldiers and a new Governor for Ormuz." This was the fleet of the new Viceroy-elect, Dom Francisco da Gama, Conde da Vidigueira, who had occupied the same post twenty-five years earlier, but these vessels were intercepted and defeated by a combined Anglo-Dutch fleet off Moçambique in July ; with the result that of the intended reinforcements for Ormuz, only the galleon *São Salvador*, commanded by Captain Gonçalo de Siqueira de Sousa, was able to reach Muscat in August.[1]   Thanks to all these disasters, the naval power of the Portuguese in India was at a very low ebb, and it was obviously impossible for Ruy Freyre and Constantino de Sá to assume the offensive with the solitary galleon and few oared vessels at their disposal. Under these circumstances, they determined to return to Goa, whither they repaired in September, leaving Dom Gonçalo da Silveira as Captain-Major of the straits of Ormuz, and in command of the scanty forces available at Muscat.

The situation of the Portuguese in the Gulf was now critical in the extreme, and had the English and Persians followed up their success with a vigorous attack on Muscat, it is difficult to see how the place could have been held. The Persians were indeed desirous of assuming the offensive, but the English, disgusted with their experience of Persian perfidy at Ormuz, flatly declined to pull their chestnuts out of the fire for the second time. The English losses during the actual

[1]This fleet consisted of the carracks *Santa Tereza, São Joseph, São Carlos, Santo Thomé*, the galleons *Trindade* and *São Salvador*, together with two pinnaces. An account of the voyage of this fleet, and its defeat by the Anglo-Dutch squadron off Moçambique, will be found in my article *Dom Francisco da Gama, Conde da Vidigueira, e a sua viagem para a India no ano de 1622*, (Lisboa, *Anais do Club militar-naval*, 1930), which is based on all available contemporary Portuguese, Dutch and English sources.

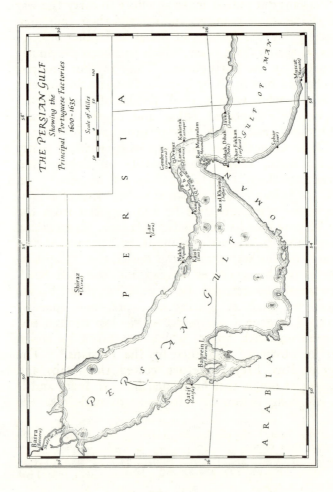

THE PERSIAN GULF
Shewing the
Principal Portuguese Factories
1600 - 1635

Scale of Miles
50   0   50   100

fighting had been very few, but it was with crews greatly decimated by sickness that Weddell and Blyth returned to Swally in September.[1] Left to themselves, the Persians did indeed make an effort to carry the war into the enemy's country, and opened their campaign by occupying the fortress of Sohar and other strongholds on the Arabian coast, which had been previously evacuated by the Portuguese. Their further progress was checked first of all by Captain Gonçalo de Siqueira de Sousa, who, with a small flotilla of seven *fustas*, temporarily recaptured Sohar and drove them back to Ormuz ; and, when they returned to the charge, by Dom Gonçalo da Silveira, who, with a vastly inferior force, routed their flotilla off Sohar, thus preventing them from advancing on Muscat.[2] In May, 1623, Ruy Freyre returned to the scene of action, with some reinforcements he had received from the new Viceroy who had dissuaded him from his intention of becoming an Augustinian monk, and persuaded him to carry on the war against the Persians as " Captain-General of the straits of Ormuz and the Red Sea." Determined to retrieve his reputation, Ruy Freyre wasted no time in getting to work, and speedily organised an expedition to recover the lost strongholds, commencing with Sohar, which was taken by storm after an obstinate resistance by the Persians.[3] The news of Ruy Freyre's return cowed the Arabs and Persians, as much as it heartened his own men, and it was not long before he felt ready to undertake the

[1]Compare Foster's *English Factories*, 1622-1623, pp. xii and xviii, and documents there cited.

[2]*Cf.* the documents printed in *Dois Capitães da India*, (Lisboa, 1898), pp. 53 flg., and Queiroz, *Vida do Irmão Pedro de Basto* (Lisboa, 1689) Livro III, Cap V, p. 277.

[3]*Commentarios*, Chapters 43 and 44. *Dois Capitães da India*, pp. 60-70. Della Valle, *Travels* (1665 edition), p. 92.

89

blockade of Ormuz. This he did to such effect, by ravaging the neighbouring Persian littoral and burning and destroying all boats which he could get hold of, that all communication with the mainland was practically severed, except for an occasional boat which could slip across to Gombrun by night. Ruy Freyre might indeed have been able to recapture the Castle, had he been properly supported from Goa; but his force was too small, lack of men and provisions compelling him to return to Muscat at the end of the year.[1] If Della Valle is to be believed, the poor support he obtained from Goa was mainly due to the jealousy of the Viceroy ; but a more probable reason was the great want of ships and men in Goa itself, the India-bound fleet which left the Tagus in 1623, having been nearly as unfortunate as its predecessors of the two previous years.[2] During his blockade of Ormuz, Ruy Freyre had made a fireship attack by night on the shipping moored under the Castle walls, which included the English ship *Reformation* and the Dutch *Heusden*, this latter vessel being the first of her nation to appear in the Gulf. This attack was only partially successful, for although some " Moorish " ships were burnt, the *Heusden* beat off the attackers and quenched the flames on board the *Reformation*, which had been seriously imperilled for a time.[3]

[1]Della Valle *Travels*, pp. 201-203.

[2]*São Francisco Xavier, Santa Izabel, Nossa Senhora da Conceição, São Simão, Misericordia, Santo André, São Braz* and the pinnace *Nossa Senhora da Guia*. Of this fleet, three vessels were wrecked and most of the others compelled to winter in Mocambique. The *Nossa Senhora da Guia* was taken by the E.I.C. ship *Coaster*, outward bound for Batavia, near the Cape, but released as being " so spoiled in the fight," which had lasted for 12 hours. The Captain was sent to Malacca, on his promising to try to effect the release of the English captives (from the *Unicorn*) detained there.

[3]*Cal. S.P. East Indies*, 1622-1624, p. 230. Terpstra, *Opkomst der Westerquartieren der O.I.C.* (Hague, 1918), pp. 151-157, q.v. for the foundation of Dutch commercial relations with Persia in 1623-1624.

At the beginning of 1624, Ruy Freyre received a request for help from the Turkish Pasha of Basra, who was being hard pressed by a strong Persian army under the command of the Imam Quli Khan, the captor of Ormuz. Adversity does indeed make strange bed-fellows, and it is curious to think that the Portuguese should now be making common cause with their hereditary enemies, the Ottoman Turks, with whom they had been at war ever since the discovery of the maritime route to India. Basra was at this time quite an important centre for the Portuguese trade in the Gulf, and, after the fall of Ormuz, had become with Muscat their principal mart. For this reason, and to divert the enemy's attention from Muscat, Ruy Freyre readily consented to the Pasha's proposal, and sent thither a force of five or six galliots under the command of Dom Gonçalo da Silveira, who was by this time Ruy Freyre's *alter ego*. Dom Gonçalo's little force proved very effective in the energetic hands of its commander, and was chiefly responsible for forcing the Imam Quli Khan to quit the invaded province in 1625. Such a thorn did it prove in the Persian's flesh, that in 1624-1625, the Khan of Shiras urgently requested the English to send some ships to Basra in support of the Persians against the Portuguese flotilla, offering to defray their expenses if necessary. The commanders bluntly rejected this offer, chiefly on the grounds that it would have involved them in war with the Turks, to the consequent detriment of English trade in the Levant. Dom Gonçalo remained at Basra until November, 1625, when he rejoined Ruy Freyre off Ormuz.[1]

[1]Foster, *English Factories, 1624-1629*, pp. 42-43. *Dois Capitães da India*, pp. 70-89. Dom Gonçalo ascended the Euphrates with this flotilla as high as Babylon on one occasion. Amongst the documents attesting the value of his services in this expedition, are some interesting translations of letters of thanks from the Pasha and the Turkish Grand Vizier. In this year the

Whilst the Persians were wasting their strength against Basra and Baghdad, Ruy Freyre, having received some reinforcements and munitions from the Viceroy, had resumed the blockade of Ormuz in August with a fleet of about thirty galliots and *terradas*, " a small preparation indeed to take Ormuz withall," as Della Valle scornfully remarks. Nevertheless, with this small force, he pressed the blockade so closely and wrought such havoc amongst Persian shipping in the Gulf, that sea-borne commerce practically ceased to exist. With trade thus almost at a standstill, the English were again earnestly pressed by the Persians to aid them, for the latter perceived that unless they were relieved by sea, Ormuz was bound to fall into the hands of Ruy Freyre sooner or later.[1] Deliverance, however, was at hand. Owing to the slackness of trade, consequent on the Portuguese blockade, only two English ships had gone to Persia in the winter of 1623, but in November, 1624 a really strong combined Anglo-Dutch fleet of ten sail lay in Swally Hole, ready to proceed thither. This display of force had been rendered necessary, not so much by the presence of Ruy Freyre's galliots off Ormuz, as by the fact that a strong squadron of fighting galleons had arrived at Goa from Lisbon in September, which, in conjunction with two other India-built vessels, was being fitted out to join Ruy Freyre's fleet at Ormuz, and make a final effort to retake the island once and for all. The fate of Ormuz depended on who got there first, and fortunately for the Persians, who were by now in a desperate condition, the race

war between Turkey and Persia had flared up again, and the Persian attack on Basra was countered by the Turks besieging Baghdad, which was however relieved by Shah Abbas in person in 1625.

[1]*Cal. S.P. East Indies*, 1622-1624, pp. 287, 442, 450-451. Foster, *English Factories*, 1624-1629, pp. 42, 80. " So as it is a misery to think what Ormuz hath been, and what it now is."

was won by the Allies. The Dutch had actually arrived first on the 23rd December, followed a few days later by the English who stood in for Ormuz "where wee met our old freinde Rufrero with 17 or 18 frigetts to keepe the Persian from landing one Armooze." Ruy Freyre could of course do nothing against such powerful ships, and was compelled to stand over to Larak in order to await the coming of the galleons, which was not long delayed.

The six galleons which had reached Goa in September under the command of the Captain-General Nuno Alvarez Botelho, "a stout and expert soldier," had gone north to join two strong India-built vessels at Bassein in December ; but owing to the delay in taking provisions on board, it was not until the 6th of January that Botelho was able to leave for the Gulf with his eight sail. Even then he was none too well supplied with water, and he had a stormy passage, in which the flagship sprung her mainmast. Such nevertheless was Botelho's eagerness to close with his enemies, that he would not put into Muscat to water or refit, but made all the sail he could to get to Ormuz as soon as possible, hoping to catch his opponents unawares. The latter however had arranged with the captain of the Persian garrison of Kishm Castle, to fire some warning guns if he should discern any " crosse sails " on the horizon ; and the discharge of the Persian cannon in the early dawn of February 10th, 1625, told them that their expected foe was at hand. No doubt the memory of Amboina was still fresh in the minds of the two North-sea races, but all differences were sunk in view of the common peril, and Anglo-Dutch co-operation during the ensuing battles left nothing to be desired.

A calm prevented the two sides from joining battle on the first day, but early next morning the action began in earnest. Full and graphic accounts of the hard-fought battles have come down to us from the pens of participants on both sides, so that only the briefest outline need be given here.[1] The Dutch squadron was first under sail, and their Admiral discharged the first shot at Botelho's flagship which " presently answered him with three for one." Weddell and the English were not far behind and on their arrival the battle became fiercer than ever, a calm supervening which enabled every shot to take effect. The action was fought at exceedingly close range, but there was only one instance of boarding, this being when the Dutch ship *Dordrecht* fell foul of the Portuguese Vice-Admiral's ship *São Francisco*, from whom she cleared herself after some hours and with the loss of her ensign,

---

[1]The best English accounts are those calendared in Foster's *English Factories,* 1624-1629, pp. 46-54 and 80-86. There is also a spirited account of the action (based on Weddell's own report) by John Taylor, the celebrated " Water-Poet," printed under the title of, *A famous fight at Sea, where foure English Ships under the command of Captaine Iohn Weddell and foure Dutch Ships fought three dayes in the Gulfe of Persia neere Ormus, against 8 Portugall Gallions and 3 Frigotts . . .* London, 1627, 4°, being afterwards included in the collected edition of Taylor's works, 1630. This narrative was subsequently reproduced by Lediard in his *Naval History of England,* (London, 1735), pp. 477-482, on which Clowes based his description of the fight in Vol. II of his *History of the British Navy.* Taylor's pamphlet has its counterpart on the Dutch side, in an equally rare little tract published at Amsterdam in 1626 under the title of *Waerachtich verhael vande victorieuse Zeestrijdt tusschen acht Portvgysche Galleonen ende vier Hollandtsche met vier Engelsche schepen omtrent Ormus ende de Persische kust voorgevallen,* etc. A practically identical account is to be found on pp. 157-160 of the *Dagh-Register gehouden in't Casteel Batavia,* 1624-1629. A contemporary Spanish pamphlet on the battle, entitled *Relacion de la Batalla que Nuno Álbarez Botello, General de la armada de altobordo, del mar de la India, tuvo con las Armadas de Olanda, y Inglaterra en el estrecho de Ormuz,* was printed by Bernadino de Guzman at Madrid in 1626, but the best account from the Iberian side is contained in the *Rellação summaria e mui verdadeira dos successos da Armada do Capitam geral Nuno Alvarez Botelho,* etc., written in December, 1625 by an Augustinian monk who was chaplain to the Armada, and first published by the present writer at Oporto in 1928 under the title of *Nuno Alvares Botelho e a sua Armada de alto-bordo,* 1624-1625, reprinted from Vol. XVI of the magazine *Historia.* A full list of the squadrons of all the contending parties will be found in this essay, together with details of their tonnage, number of guns and so forth. An annotated English translation of the *Rellação Summaria* is to be found on pp. 231-248 of the English edition of Ruy Freyre's *Commentaries,* op. cit.

by the help of the *James*. The Dutch commander, Albard Becker, having been killed early on in the action, his ship fell off to leeward, and her place was taken by Weddell in the *James*, who carried on a murderous duel with Botelho's galleon, *São Francisco Xavier* at very close range. When the action was at its height, Ruy Freyre d'Andrade came on the scene with three galliots, and Botelho, not recognising him, ordered him to get out a hawser and try to tow the head of his galleon round, so that he might board the *James*. This Ruy Freyre was about to do, when Botelho, being told of his identity, went into the beak-head of his ship, and called out apologies to Ruy Freyre who was standing on the poop of his galliot. In this posture the two courtly fidalgos remained for some time, exchanging mutual compliments whilst exposed to the concentrated fire of the enemy, before they could be induced to withdraw to less perilous positions by their anxious followers. The dauntless behaviour of Ruy Freyre and Botelho greatly encouraged their men, who responded unflinchingly to the withering fire of the Anglo-Dutch squadron, whose crews likewise fought so cheerfully " that sartane Portugalls wich wee had formerly taken, being then in cheanes, tould us wee fought as though it had bine a Maye game, not dreding nor regarding our lives in so good a cause." In this manner the fight continued, " very hot, fearce and cruel," until sheer exhaustion parted the combatants at sunset.

The Portuguese casualties in men and material during the first day's action had been very severe, many of their senior officers having been slain, but their morale was still unimpaired. The indefatigable Botelho visited each vessel during the night, heartening the crews, supervising repairs, and appointing fresh captains and commanders in place of those killed or disabled. Amongst those severely wounded was the Rear-Admiral, Antonio Telles, whose galleon on the next morning (Ash Wednesday) " rowled by the board her maine topmast, with part of her mainemast, and alsoe her foretopmast."[1] Although thus crippled by the loss of his strongest ship, Botelho did not hesitate to accept the challenge of the allied squadron, which, having refreshed and refitted themselves at Gombrun, bore down upon him at dawn on February 13th.

This second day's fight " continued as bludy as it was at the first," or even more so, " the sea being all as callme and smooth as the Themes and wee continually bord and bord." The English concentrated their efforts on Botelho's flagship to begin with, but the Portuguese " behaved themselves very stoutly." A prize renamed the *John* had been fitted up as a fireship, one Darby being placed in command, with the promise of £100 reward if he clapped his ship alongside the *São Francisco Xavier*. But the Portuguese were on the alert, and Ruy Freyre with three frigates succeeded in isolating this vessel from the fleet, and she had perforce to be set alight prematurely and abandoned in order to avoid capture. In the afternoon, the allied squadron succeeded in surrounding the galleon *Trindade* commanded by Francisco de Souza de Castro, which was almost entirely disabled owing to damage received

---

[1] A contemporary English account states that the *São Sebastião* " had been built upon a carrack at Cochin [alias Damão] only for to make a battery and to be a barracado to the rest of her fleet. She was saker, if not whole culverin proof in her lower works. This ship did more spoile unto our fleet than any three of their ships taken together." Her captain, Antonio Telles, had later a distinguished career, for he subsequently rose to be Captain-General of the galleons, 1636-1639 (in which capacity he had three pitched battles with the blockading Dutch squadrons off Goa's bar); Governor of India from 1639-1640 (when he was on excellent terms with the English at Surat, who described him as " our worthie friend "); Captain-General of the Home fleet in 1641-1657; Governor of Brazil from 1647-1650, and finally appointed Viceroy of India in 1657, when he died on the outward voyage to Goa.

in masts, hull and rudder. This unfortunate vessel was so mishandled that out of her crew of 250 men only seven or eight survived ; but despite this phenomenal punishment she did not surrender, and was eventually relieved by Botelho's flagship.[1] By this time both sides were thoroughly exhausted and at sunset the English " ware so faint and werey that our men began to drop downe for very faintness." The Portuguese were in like condition, or even worse, and so once more nightfall parted the combatants on equal terms.

At the end of this action the Portuguese were in a sorry plight. Their losses had been extremely heavy, the casualties in the flagship alone amounting to over sixty, and though the allies had by no means escaped scatheless, they had the port of Gombrun in which to refit and replenish their supplies of food and ammunition at leisure.[2] The galleons had all suffered severely in their hulls and rigging, and were in urgent need of

[1]Taylor's pamphlet (on the authority of a French deserter) states that out of 250 men in the *Trindade*, 243 were slain in this second day's fight. Laird Clowes (*Royal Navy*, Vol. II) remarks that this must be a misprint or an exaggeration, but the statement is confirmed by a contemporary Portuguese source, *Jornada que Francisco de Sousa de Castro . . . fez ao Achem, com uma importante Embaixada, enviado pelo Visorei da India Pedro da Silva, no anno de* 1638, (Goa, 1642, (reprinted in the *Levantamento de Ximabara*, etc., Lisboa, 1643), whose author, Frei Gonsalo de São José, states he was an eye-witness of this heroic feat. Francisco de Souza de Castro was in later years Captain of Damão, where he was on excellent terms with the English. His name is often mentioned in the documents calendared in Foster's *English Factories*, 1630-1641. Whilst he was a prisoner in the hands of the treacherous Achinese in 1638-1640, the English tried to secure his release, but in vain.

[2]The expenditure of ammunition on both sides was colossal. The *James* fired 550 shot the first day, and 1,112 the second, whilst Botelho's flagship expended 1,500 shot in this last action alone. The English and Persians ashore in Gombrun estimated the total number of cannon balls fired at 16,000 on the first day and 17,000 on the second ! In view of this prodigious expenditure of ammunition, most of it at close range, the English and Dutch losses were surprisingly low, amounting to less than 80 slain all told, whereas the *James* alone had received over 400 shot during the fights. The Portuguese losses were much heavier, but over half of them occurred in the luckless *Trindade*, whilst the *São Francisco Xavier*, Botelho's flagship, had 84 killed and wounded in the two days' fight.

repair, whilst there was no port with dockyard facilities any nearer than Muscat. Furthermore, the shortage of water had by now become acute, whilst the ships were crowded with dead and wounded. Despite all these unfavourable circumstances, however, Botelho refused to be cowed, and the most he would consent to do was to sail across to the anchorage in the neighbouring islet of Larak, where he anchored to await the departure of the Anglo-Dutch squadron from Gombrun. In taking this decision he was supported by Ruy Freyre d'Andrade and the acting Vice-Admiral, Dom Francisco Coutinho, against the practically unanimous opinion of all the other captains of the armada.[1]

The allies had refrained from attacking Botelho in his refuge, since they knew their foe to be " implacable, malicious and politique," or, in other words, very good enemies, as Laird Clowes observes. They busied themselves with taking on board their cargoes, and refitting their ships as best they could. Meanwhile, the Persians were desperately anxious to persuade them to stay and help them against the Portuguese ; but this the Dutch refused to do on any terms, whilst the English did not consider themselves strong enough to do so alone, although the Governor of Gombrun offered them a bribe of 500 *Tūmans* a month if they would do so. Accordingly the allied squadron put out to sea on February 23rd with fourteen sail, including three Indian vessels, and carrying two Persian Ambassadors destined for England and Holland respectively.[2]

[1] Dom Francisco Coutinho had come from Goa to join Ruy Freyre's squadron, in the same galliot in which Della Valle was travelling to Basra. The Italian traveller is loud in his praises of the conduct and courage of Dom Francisco ; and that these praises were amply justified is proved by the courage displayed by him not only on this occasion, but in later years against the Dutch off Malacca. (Della Valle, *Travels*, Chapter X, pp. 235-239.)

[2] Naqd Ali Beg in the *Star* for England, whence he returned with Sir Robert Sherley in 1627 ; and Musa Beg in the *Maagd van Dort* for Holland, whence he likewise returned in the same year.

The Portuguese made sail at the same time and kept ahead of the allied squadron all night, when the weather freshened and Ruy Freyre's galliots were compelled to return to Larak, having first sent some soldiers on board the galleons as reinforcements. At noon on the 24th, the allies came up with the Portuguese, who had shortened sail to wait for them, when both sides " fell to it pell mell, our ordnance gowinge off as fast as smalle shott." During this action the English concentrated all their efforts on Botelho's flagship, " not so much looking after or heeding the other ships," but the Portuguese commander did not flinch from his station, until he was eventually relieved by Antonio Telles in the *São Sebastião*, which " crept in betwixt the *James* and the Portugall Admirall, lying as a Bulwarke to weather off her, to receive all that might be put upon her, and indeed all that was meant to have been bestowed upon the Admirall was still plyed upon that great Hulke." The scene of this battle was some six leagues to the South-east of Cape Musandam ; and the fight whilst it lasted was the hottest of the three, " and hotter it would have proved, had not the approaching darkness of the unwelcome night cryed a requiem to our bloudy resolutions." By this time both sides were short of ammunition, and neither being anxious to have " t'other odd bout," they stood away on their respective courses, the English for Swally and the Portuguese for Muscat.

Needless to say, both sides were loud in their claims of victory after the last of these memorable actions had been fought, but whether any real advantage was gained by either party is more than doubtful. The allied squadron had undoubtedly inflicted far heavier losses on their opponents, both in men and material, than they had received, and thus far they could claim a tactical success. But on the other hand, the Portuguese had for the first (and last) time really held their own in the face of an equal, or even slightly superior opponent at sea, and their morale was no whit impaired by the hammering they had received. In these battles they had regained that confidence in themselves which they had lost after Ruy Freyre's defeats off Jask in 1621 ; and for the first time since the appearance of the Anglo-Dutch fleets in Eastern waters, they had given battle on equal terms without losing a ship or being driven off the scene of action in confusion. For this result they had Nuno Alvarez Botelho to thank, and him alone. Thanks to his dauntless courage, indefatigable zeal and dogged perseverance, he had inspired his men with much of his own spirit ; and they followed and fought for him even more willingly than they did for the equally gallant, but harsher spirited Ruy Freyre. Botelho had taken special care before leaving Goa, to have as many Europeans and as few half-castes or natives as possible amongst his crews, whilst he also paid special attention to securing competent gunners and sailors—points usually neglected by the average Portuguese captain, who thought only of filling his ship with a horde of ill-disciplined and sea-sick soldiers. So high, indeed, was the quality of his crews, that both English and Dutch refused to believe that they were Portuguese, and alleged they must be mainly " English, Scotch, Irish and Dutch runnagadoes." [1]

For the moment the initiative in the Gulf was in the hands of the Portuguese, and the question now arose as to what use to make of Botelho's armada. At a full council meeting, called by the Viceroy in Goa to

[1]Foster's, *English Factories*, 1624-1629, p. 50. Manoel Xavier, S. J., *Historia do Governador da India, Nuno Alvarez Botelho*, (Lisboa, 1633), pp. 80-81. It is amusing to note that the English made similar and equally unfounded statements, after the heroic stand made by Dom Manoel de Menezes in the *São Julião* in a three days fight against four English ships off the Comoro islands in 1616.

discuss this matter, two points of view were put forward. The first of these was that the galleons should come and cruise off the West coast of India in September, in order to lay in wait for the outward-bound Anglo-Dutch Indiamen off Swally ; whilst the contrary view was that they should stay in the Gulf to assist Ruy Freyre, who otherwise would not have sufficient men and munitions to undertake the siege of Ormuz with any prospect of success. After long and earnestly debating the point, it was decided to leave the decision in the hands of Botelho and Ruy Freyre at Muscat ; and this information was sent by the six sail under the command of Gaspar Gomes, which left for Muscat on April 11th, 1625, with large supplies of money, provisions, timber and munitions for the Armada.[1]

The council of war convened to debate the matter at Muscat, finally decided by a majority vote in favour of Ruy Freyre's view that the galleons should proceed to Swally in September, there to waylay the English and Dutch Indiamen, as if these were prevented from sailing to the Gulf, the fall of Ormuz was bound to follow sooner or later ; whilst there would not be time for Botelho's galleons to join Ruy Freyre in blockading Ormuz, and then proceed to India to intercept the outward-bound allied shipping. Botelho himself was of a contrary opinion, and offered to serve as a volunteer with 600 musketeers from his crew under Ruy Freyre's command in the siege, before sailing for Swally in September, whence he calculated he could return to the Gulf in November after defeating the English and Dutch.[2] All his captains however sided with Ruy

[1]Letter of the Conde da Vidigueira, Goa, 29/ii/1626, in Livro das Monções, no. 22 fls. 114-119. The reinforcements were conveyed in two galleons São Pedro and São Salvador, two carracks and two pinnaces.

[2]Letter of the Conde da Vidigueira, Goa, 29/ii/1626. Among the Egerton Manuscript in the British Museum, are two letters written by Botelho

Freyre, whose estimate of the time factor was undoubtedly correct; and it was therefore resolved that Botelho should sail for Swally as soon as possible, leaving Ruy Freyre to resume the blockade of Ormuz with his flotilla of galliots and other oared vessels.

It was typical of Botelho's noble character, that although his own opinion had been overruled, he threw himself heart and soul into the work of refitting his shattered vessels; labouring himself incessantly from morning till night, and not ceasing work even in the appalling noon-day heat of Muscat, which has probably the hottest climate in the world. Fired by his example, the men worked with a will, but two of the galleons, *São Sebastião* and *Trindade*, were too badly damaged to be able to be repaired with the scanty resources available at Muscat, and were sent back to Goa in advance. Botelho followed with the remainder at the first opportunity, but his squadron was separated by a storm at the entrance to the Gulf, as a result of which three galleons, *Misericordia, Santo Antonio* and *Santiago*, were driven ashore near Bombay, though most of their crews and artillery were saved.[1]

Although thus weakened by the unexpected loss of three of his vessels, and the temporary absence of two others, Botelho took up his station with his four

---

to some prominent minister (? Olivares) at Madrid, dated off Ormuz on February 22nd, and at Muscat on May 29th respectively. In the former one he hints that he would like to be given the order of the Golden Fleece, and the Captaincy-General of the Portuguese home fleet, whilst in the latter he expresses his disgust at the way in which his claims have been ignored, in the picturesque phrase, " *Emfim señor, triste el Pastor qne en triste valle naçe.*"

[1]*Idem. Cf.* also the only contemporary printed account of this year's maritime events in India, from the Portuguese side, as contained in the excessively rare pamphlet (of which I know of no other copy in existence save my own) entitled : *Carta e Relaçam dos successos do Estado da India desde o principio do anno de 1625, e o de 1626, ate quatorze de fevereiro, que as Naos partirão pera o Reyno. Com tudo o mais que sucedeo a Nuno Alvarez Botelho, & a Rui Freire d'Andrade, & mais Armadas que sahirão, & o que fizerão,* [at end]. Em Lisboa. Pedro Craesbeeck. Anno 1626.

remaining storm-tossed galleons off Swally, where six powerful English and Dutch vessels lay in the " Hole." The moral superiority established by Botelho, as a result of his fights in the Persian Gulf in February, was clearly evidenced by the fact that the allies would not venture to come out and fight him, though publicly challenged to do so " shippe to shippe or all together," Botelho even offering to stand off and give them sea room if necessary.[1] Not only so, but when on the 17th October, three outward-bound English ships, *Lion, Palsgrave* and *Dolphin*, hove in sight and Botelho stood out to sea to attack them, the ships at Swally " most basely lay still," though had they come out, the odds against the Portuguese would have been nearly two to one. Botelho in his flagship, and Gaspar Gomes in the *São Pedro*, eventually overhauled the *Lion* which was a " slug," and clapped her aboard one on each quarter, the *Palsgrave* and *Dolphin* making no effort to relieve their consort, but continuing their flight with all sails set. The Portuguese now swarmed aboard the *Lion* and were speedily masters of her poop and upper deck, whilst the frigate flotilla had now come up, whose men threw firepots in at the ports and stuck fire-pikes in her sides. The situation appeared desperate, when the English by dropping an anchor at the stern, and the tide running very strong, brought the ship up so suddenly that the Portuguese cables and grappling irons were broken, and the

[1]Botelho's galleons were the *São Francisco Xavier, São Francisco, São Pedro* and *São Salvador,* accompanied by some 14 or 15 frigates or light oared craft. The English ships were the *Jonas, Anne* and *Scout,* whilst the Dutch vessels included the *Goude Leeuw, Heusden* and *Walcheren.* A translation of Botelho's public defiance to the Anglo-Dutch commanders, which was nailed by his orders to the gates of the chief public buildings in Surat, will be found on pp. 248-249 of the English edition of the *Commentaries.* Both English and Dutch blamed each other for not venturing out. The English side is given in Foster's 1624-1629 volume *op. cit.*, and the Dutch version in the journal of Pieter van den Broeck, head of the Netherlands Factory at Surat, as printed in Volume II of the *Begin ende Voortgangh,* (Amsterdam, 1646).

galleons, drifting on with the fast flowing current, were soon lost to sight in the darkness. Fifty or sixty Portuguese boarders still remained on the poop, and as these could not be dislodged, a barrel of gunpowder was placed aft under the deck, and the Portuguese " blown to their parent the devill." [1] Meanwhile Botelho, thinking that the *Lion* must be either burnt or sunk, left only five frigates by her. to complete the work of destruction, and passed on with his remaining vessels in pursuit of the *Palsgrave* and *Dolphin*, which he soon overhauled and hotly engaged for two days, until finally the two English vessels escaped by altering their course in the night, and steering due south for the Comoro islands. The commanders of the frigates left to watch the *Lion* lost their heads at this juncture, and so she was able to resume her voyage, crippled as she was, and eventually reached Gombrun where she was repaired as well as the limited facilities of that place would permit.

Ruy Freyre with his galliots was still engaged in the blockade of Ormuz, and on hearing of the *Lion's* arrival he prepared to attack her. He did not have long to wait, for the factors on shore in consultation with the Master considered the roadstead of Gombrun to be too exposed, and ordered the ship to take refuge beneath the walls of Ormuz Castle. On the morning of November 18th as the *Lion* was preparing to weigh anchor, Ruy Freyre came rowing towards her with about 15 sail of frigates. A contemporary English writer had contemptuously stated on one occasion, that such frigates or galliots, " were no more to be regarded than butterflies," but although powerless against capital ships when there was a wind to manoeuvre with, they could be very dangerous in a calm, when

[1] The *Carta e Relaçam* asserts that all these men were picked up out of the sea by the frigates.

commanded by an officer of the courage and experience of Ruy Freyre. So it proved on this occasion, for Ruy Freyre so handled his flotilla that the *Lion* could only make use of her bow and stern pieces, and his frigates so pestered her with hand-grenades, powder-pots and musketry fire, that the English were not able to open a port in the ship, " but were forced to shoot away, ports and all." Finally, the upper deck collapsed on the heads of the gun-crews, " who seeing death on each side, some leaped overboard, and put themselves to the mercy of their enemies, the rest gave fire to the Powder-roome, and blew up the ship." The Portuguese gave quarter to the survivors swimming about in the water, but Ruy Freyre made an indelible stain on his own honour by executing all of them save one, the next day. The fortunate survivor was Thomas Winterborne, the ship's cook, who owed his life to the special kindness with which he had treated Ruy Freyre during his captivity on board the *Lion* in 1622 ; and who was now set on shore with the heads of his twenty-six comrades wrapped up in silk, and a letter from Ruy Freyre to the factors at Gombrun, explaining that this barbarous act was a reprisal for the execution of the Lascarins handed over by the English to the Persians after the fall of Kishm, contrary to the articles of surrender then agreed upon.[1]

Whilst this tragedy was being enacted off Gombrun, Botelho's galleons, all of which had received a good deal of damage in their masts and hulls from the fire of the fleeing *Palsgrave* and *Dolphin*, were busy refitting in Bombay road, whither they had sailed on the 28th

[1]See the account as related in Taylor's pamphlet *op. cit.*, and the Portuguese versions in the *Commentaries* and *Carta e Relacam.* For English indignation over Ruy Freyre's wanton barbarity, compare remarks in the English edition of *Commentaries*, p. 312. The English lost 68 men in this action, whilst the Portuguese losses were seven killed and twenty wounded, according to their own account.

October. The allied ships in Swally had belatedly put to sea on the 20th, too late to help their consorts ; and three other Dutch vessels from Batavia under the command of Frederic Cistiens, which passed Botelho's squadron off Bombay on the 28th, likewise avoided an engagement. Botelho remained overhauling his vessels at Bombay until January, 1626, when he was reinforced by the galleons *São Sebastião*, *São Ieronimo* and *Reis Magos*, carrying 550 men and 80 guns, commanded by Antonio Telles who had been sent by the Viceroy from Goa on the 22nd December, 1625. Meanwhile the joint Anglo-Dutch fleet of ten ships sailed for Persia at the beginning of December,[1] and on their return to Swally in February, 1626, they found in the road another four sail of Dutch vessels under Herman Van Speult, which had just arrived from Batavia.[2]

There were now some fifteen English and Dutch ships at Swally, and in view of this overwhelming force, the position of Botelho's seven galleons at Bombay gave rise to great anxiety in the minds of the Viceroy and his council at Goa. It had been originally intended to send the armada to Muscat to protect that stronghold from an expected Anglo-Dutch attack, but this idea had been given up when it was heard that Ruy Freyre had withdrawn there from Ormuz on the appearance of the combined squadron in the Gulf at the end of 1625.[3] The next plan was to use

[1]*James, Jonas, Anne* and *Falcon* under the command of Captain Weddell for the English, and *Goede Fortuijn, Bantam, Engelsche Beer, Gouden Leeuw, Walcheren* and *Heusden* under Cistiens for the Dutch. Weddell's orders for the voyage, and an account of it, will be found in the documents calendared on pp. 105-117 of Foster's *English Factories, 1624-1629.*

[2]*Mauritius, Oranje, Hollandia* and a prize. It will be recalled that Van Speult was the man responsible for the " massacre " of Amboina, but he seems to have been on good terms with Weddell, although Kerridge and the Surat factors protested against his appointment.

[3]Viceroy's letter, Goa, 26/ii/1626. The Anglo-Dutch threat against Muscat did not materialise, although the Persians frequently broached the

the galleons for cruising off Swally to intercept outward-bound Indiamen, but this idea was likewise abandoned in view of the strength of the allied squadron, and the fact that the whole naval might of the Portuguese in India was concentrated in Botelho's armada ; and it was finally resolved that the galleons should cruise off the straits of Bab-el-Mandib, at the entrance to the Red Sea, with the double object of picking up some profitable prizes, and of avoiding a battle with the greatly superior enemy fleet. They were to remain off the Red Sea until May, when they were to go to Muscat or to Tiwai for supplies, and thence to the West coast of India in September, in order to surprise and capture the isolated outward bound Indiamen, which were due to arrive at Swally in that season.[1]

In fulfilment of this plan of campaign, Botelho left Bombay for the Red Sea shortly after having been reinforced by an additional galleon, the *Santo André*, from Goa, thus bringing the strength of his squadron up to eight sail.[2] There had been some talk amongst the allied commanders of attacking and destroying Botelho's squadron as it lay in Bombay road, " so their was pretence of exsecution of it, but as smoke it vanisht, thoughe of English and Dutch we wear 14 ships and pineses."[3] Botelho's galleons cruised off

---

suggestion. Ruy Freyre received two ships from Goa with munitions in November.

[1]Viceroy's letter, *op. cit.*

[2]*São Francisco Xavier* (flagship), *São Francisco, São Sebastião, São Salvador, São Jeronimo, Reis Magos, São Pedro* and *Santo André*.

[3]Foster *op. cit.*, p. 117. The allied fleet was composed of the *James, Jonas, Anne, Falcon, Spy* (English), and the *Gouden Leeuw, Oranje, Hollandia, Mauritius, Goede Fortuyn, Beer, Walcheren, Bantam* and *Heusden* (Dutch). The English laid the blame for the failure of the expedition to materialise on the faint-heartedness of " Butcher Speult " (Foster, pp. 117-137) ; but the Dutch attribute it to want of enthusiasm on the part of the English. (McLeod : *De Oost-Indische Compagnie als Zeemogendheid in Azie*, (Rijswijk, 1928), p. 418).

the mouth of the straits of Bab-el-Mandib until the end of April, when they left for Muscat as originally planned ; they thus just missed encountering an equal number of Dutch ships, which had sailed for Mocha at the beginning of the month under the command of Herman Van Speult who died there. From Muscat, where Ruy Freyre was busy strengthening the fortifications, they sailed for the West coast of India in September, " and being nowe but six shipps, discrying the Dutch a day before their coming in with the land, used their best endeavour to have encountered them ; which the Dutch (having advantage of winde) in regard of their laden shipps avoided, though provoked by sundry challenging shott from the enemies admirall." Botelho having thus failed to bring the Dutch to action, stood in for Damão, and on hearing that the outward-bound English fleet had reached Swally early in October, he sailed with his galleons for Diu. Meanwhile, the allied commanders at Swally had revived the idea of an expedition against Bombay, whither they proceeded with twelve sail, hoping to trap Botelho in the harbour, being unaware that he had gone for Diu. Being baulked of their expected prey, they landed a force which burnt and sacked what little property there was on shore, and then returned to Swally, content with this somewhat barren exploit.[1]

In December, 1626, another strong Anglo-Dutch fleet of eleven sail left for the Gulf in order " to prosecute the Persian trade." [2] They half expected to meet with the Portuguese galleons, and the English factors in their letters home, bitterly complained of

[1]Detailed contemporary accounts of the sack of Bombay are to be found in Foster, *op. cit.*, pp. 142 flg. An account from the Portuguese side in Faria y Sousa, *Asia Portugueza*, Vol. III.

[2]*Palsgrave, Dolphin, William, Blessing, Discovery* and *Morris* (English), and the *Zierickzee, Wapen van Zeelandt, Mauritius, Hollandia* and *Engelsche Beer* (Dutch).

the hampering effect of the presence of Botelho's squadron, whose mere existence forced the English and Dutch to sail in company with each other, and even then in large fleets. Nothing was seen of the galleons however, and in fact Portuguese shipping in the Gulf was limited to a little flotilla of eight oared vessels under Dom Gonçalo da Silveira, who was cruising off Ormuz ; Ruy Freyre himself being still busy with the remainder of his armada at Muscat. Accordingly the English and Dutch returned safely to Swally in March, 1627, after rejecting the annual Persian proposal for an attack on Muscat.

During the whole of the year 1626, Ruy Freyre had been busily employed in strengthening the fortifications at Muscat, and, in accordance with the orders of the Viceroy at Goa, he had not resumed the siege of Ormuz. Early in 1627 it was resolved to make a great effort to capture that stronghold before the appearance of the English and Dutch ships in December ; and accordingly Botelho with his galleons left for Muscat in May of this year, in order to co-operate with Ruy Freyre in the intended siege. There is every likelihood that this expedition would have been successful, but for the fact that Botelho's squadron was shattered and partially destroyed by a terrible storm which it encountered on the 29th May, 1627. Three of Botelho's galleons were lost with all hands in the raging seas, whilst his own flagship and the remainder struggled into Tiwai completely dismasted and practically in a sinking condition.[1] From Tiwai the

[1]Father Manoel Xavier, S. J., in his *Historia do Governador da India Nuno Alvarez Botelho*, (Lisboa, 1633) has much to say of his heroic conduct on this occasion. For fifteen days his galleon drifted at the mercy of the waves, whilst the pumps and bails had to be kept going incessantly in order to keep the water-logged vessel from foundering. Both food and water supplies ran short, scores of men dying from sheer thirst, whilst others went raving mad and leapt overboard. On finally sighting land at Cape Ras al Hadd, the crew clamoured that the ship should be run ashore, but Botelho rallied their spirits and at length brought his ship to Tiwai.

shattered hulks were towed to Muscat by Ruy Freyre's frigates, but any attempt to besiege Ormuz with such depleted forces was obviously doomed to failure, and the proposed expedition was abandoned. By way of compensation it was decided to despatch a flotilla to the help of the Sheikh of Qatif who was hard-pressed by the Persians, and anxious to make a diversion against their valuable pearl fisheries at Bahrein. Accordingly Ruy Freyre and Dom Gonçalo united their forces off Qatif at the end of July, and proceeded to ravage the neighbouring Persian coasts with fire and sword, in the approved ruthless style affected by the Portuguese. These operations were continued until September when Ruy Freyre returned to Muscat, leaving Dom Gonçalo with six sail to continue the blockade of Bahrein in co-operation with the Sheikh of Qatif.[1]

The news of the partial destruction of Botelho's armada was thankfully received by the English and Dutch, so that for the first time since 1624, their Persia fleets ventured to sail separately for Gombrun, where eleven sail of allied shipping was assembled in the roadstead by the middle of January, 1628.[2] The news of this powerful concentration naturally alarmed Ruy Freyre, who feared lest it should be employed in an attack against Muscat, as the Persians confidently

[1]Documents printed on pp. 105-120 of *Dois Capitães da India*. The orders issued by Ruy Freyre for this expedition are worth reading, as they show his tactical and administrative abilities in organizing punitive expeditions of this kind. His insistence on the importance of maintaining strict discipline is also noteworthy, although, to judge from Della Valle, his captains did not always pay due heed to these injunctions.

[2]The *William, Exchange, Hart* and *Star* (English), and the *Groot Mauritius, 's Lands Mauritius, Noort Hollandt, 't Gulde Zeepaert, Bommel, Weesp* and *Nieuwicheit* (Dutch), the latter under the command of Willem Janszoon, ex-Governor of Banda. Sir Robert Sherley returned to Persia from England in this fleet, accompanied by Sir Dodmore Cotton as envoy from James I to Shah Abbas. Both of these ambassadors died at Qazvin in July of this year.

announced. He therefore resolved to muster all his resources to meet the expected assault, and accordingly recalled Dom Gonçalo da Silveira from Qatif at the end of February.[1] With this reinforcement and the four remaining galleons of Botelho, which had by now been refitted, the Portuguese were in a condition to offer a formidable resistance to any force which the allies could bring against them. In actual fact, however, there was no serious intention on the part of the enemy to attack Muscat, although the English factors at Gombrun admitted " having from our own masters advices reported both to the King and Chaun that wee should expect to the nomber of 6 or 7 shipps purposelie designed by them for the surprize of Muskatt ; " although they candidly added that they saw " no possibillitie for the attempting of anything ourselves and, when the Hollanders shall goe more roundlie to worke, as little hope of preventing them." The Dutch likewise had no particular inclination to pit their strength against Ruy Freyre's massive fortifications for the sake of the Persians' *beaux yeux*, and thus the project was once more allowed to lapse. The allied fleets returned to Swally in February, followed some weeks later by Botelho's galleons which had remained at Muscat until the menace of the expected attack was over.

With the final departure of Botelho's galleons, the Portuguese had tacitly abandoned all hope of re-capturing Ormuz by force of arms, and the remainder of the story of Anglo-Portuguese rivalry in the Gulf is soon told. As the English and Dutch were unaware

---

[1] The original order recalling Dom Gonçalo, signed by Ruy Freyre, and dated 20/ii/1628, is in the possession of the present writer, who reproduced the signature in facsimile on page 112 of the English edition of the *Commentaries*. The letter itself was reproduced by Senhor Frazão de Vasconcelos, in *Historia e Arqueologia*, (Lisboa, 1921).

that Botelho had returned to Goa, their Persian fleets sailed in company for Gombrun at the beginning of 1629, prepared to encounter the galleons in the Gulf. Needless to say nothing materialised, and the allied ships were back at Swally by the end of March.[1]

The year 1629 likewise passed without any important alteration in the position of the contending parties in the Persian Gulf, and the annual Persia fleets of the English and Dutch Companies came and went at the end of the year without any molestation from the Portuguese.[2] As a matter of fact, these latter were now busy elsewhere, for the Rajah of Achin had besieged Malacca with one of the most powerful expeditions ever sent against that battle-scarred stronghold; and although the besieging fleet and army was annihilated by Nuno Alvarez Botelho's relieving force in December, the absence of the Portuguese commander on this expedition prevented any effective aid being sent to Muscat from Goa, and compelled Ruy Freyre to limit his operations to harassing Persian coastal shipping in the Gulf.

So successful was the effect of Ruy Freyre's destructive raids, that by this time the Persians were thoroughly exhausted, and early in 1630 they made overtures for peace. The death of Shah Abbas at the beginning of 1629 may have had something to do with this weakening Persian attitude, although his successor,

---

[1] *Jonah, Hart, Christopher, Expedition, Hopewell, Eagle* and *James* (English), accompanied by the four Dutch ships *Zeepaert, Brouwershaven, Negapatam* and *Zeeburgh*, with the returning Persian Ambassador, Musa Beg. At the end of December, 1628, the President and Council at Surat had reported that " The Portugall forces are incerten, neither do wee knowe where they lye." Actually, Botelho was cruising in the galleon *Conceição* off Goa and the ilhas Queimadas, to protect local shipping from possible attacks by the Dutch or English. He remained on this station from October, 1628, till mid-January 1629. (*Dois Capitães da India*, p. 120-121.)

[2] *Charles, Discovery, Reformation* and *Jonas* (English) and *Tholen, Brouwershaven, Buren, Bommel* and *Weesp* (Dutch).

Shah Safi, had commenced his reign well enough by breaking up the Turkish siege of Baghdad. Still, the Ottoman pressure on the western frontier of Persia was a constant menace, and the fortune of war did not always favour Persian arms. In any case negotiations were opened by the Khan of Shiras, and an agreement was speedily arrived at, whereby the Portuguese were to be allowed to trade at the port of Kung on the same terms as the English at Gombrun. This agreement provided for the establishment of an agency (or " factory " in seventeenth century parlance) in the port, with a resident Factor who was empowered to issue passes to native vessels, and to receive a moiety of all Customs dues on behalf of the King of Portugal. It was further agreed that Kung should remain open to trade and commerce, even though the two parties should recommence hostilities in the Gulf at a later date—a somewhat curious stipulation, but one which was in fact observed. Ruy Freyre further endeavoured to secure exemption from attack by Dutch or English vessels, of all ships trading to Kung under protection of the Portuguese flag or passes ; but in this, naturally enough, he was unsuccessful.[1] The question of

[1] The conditions under which Ruy Freyre established the factory at Kung, are mentioned in Foster, *English Factories*, 1630-1633, p. 140, and *Dagh-Register* of Batavia for 1630-1634, p. 40. A very confused, rambling and unreliable account is given in Chapters 47 and 48 of the *Commentaries*, in which the foundation of the factory is placed *before* the fights of February, 1625, instead of five years later. Another Portuguese source, the *Diario* of the Conde de Linhares, written at Goa in 1634, states that the truce was made for six months in the year only, hostilities to be continued during the other half. There is the following curious reference to this treaty, contained in a contemporary translation of a letter from the Viceroy Dom Pedro de Almeida, written to King Charles II in November, 1677, *à propos* of Anglo-Portuguese boundary disputes near Bombay : ". . . in Persia since the loss of Ormuz, we never have had peace with that King, but for the port of Congo, by an accord made forty years agoe by General Ruy Brother (*sic*) of Andrade, with promise to pay half duty to this custom ho'use, and never to give passport except for this only port." (*Public Record Office, C.O.* 77, Vol. XIII, folio 278, reproduced in Khan, *Journal of Indian History*, Vol. I, Part III, September, 1922, p. 548.)

Ormuz was allowed to lapse for the moment, but by way of compensation Ruy Freyre founded and garrisoned a small fort at Julfar, on the Arabian shore opposite Kishm island, which was a strategic centre of some importance as well as the site of a valuable pearl fishery.

On the conclusion of this truce with Persia, Ruy Freyre's forces were free to be used elsewhere than in the Gulf, and he soon received a summons from the new Viceroy, Dom Miguel de Noronha, Conde de Linhares, to join him in an expedition that was being fitted out at Goa for a secret destination, which rumour variously reported to be the English ships at Swally, the Dutch fort Geldria at Paliacat on the Coromandel coast, and Malacca. On receipt of these orders, Ruy Freyre sailed with eight well-appointed galliots for Bassein, which he reached in November. The news of his arrival caused considerable alarm amongst the English at Swally, who had not forgotten the fate of the *Lion*, but his force was too small to effect anything. Although he put in an appearance off the " Hole," together with fourteen other frigates, he soon saw that there was no chance of taking the English by surprise, and so continued on his voyage to Goa, where he arrived on December 21st, 1630.[1] Here he remained until May, 1631, when he was sent back to Muscat by the Viceroy, since the proposed expedition against Paliacat had been abandoned on receipt of the news of Botelho's death off Jambi in the previous year, and the destruction of Constantino de Sá with his army in Ceylon. Despite Ruy Freyre's

[1]Compare documents calendared in Foster, *op. cit.*, pp. 57, 60, 97 and 100. The *Commentaries* give the date of Ruy Freyre's arrival at Goa as the 2nd February, 1631, but this is obviously wrong. Father Manoel Xavier, S. J., who was an eye-witness gives the date stated in the text, which agrees with the English statements that Ruy Freyre was off Swally during the first week in December.

absence from the Gulf, the English felt nervous about the possibility of their ships being intercepted if they should sail separately, and accordingly both their homeward-bound and Persia ships sailed together early in January for Gombrun, whence the latter returned in April having parted with their homeward-bound consorts off Jask.[1]

Ruy Freyre did not remain idle after returning to his post, for the English factors at Gombrun reported that during 1631, " Ruy Freery reigning [ranging] with three gallions and 20 frigotts in the Gulph, presented the Duke [Khan of Shiras] with 600 tomans and required the restitution of Ormus ; or if not that, then the free custom of all goods that the Portugalls should land in all places or ports there, and free trade without molestacion of the English or Dutch ; all was denied them." At the end of the same year, he detached four well-equipped galliots, manned with picked crews, to join a force of 20 frigates from Goa, which had been sent to recapture the fortress of Mombasa, taken by a sudden outbreak of the native and Arab population, after all the Portuguese inhabitants had been massacred to a man.[2]

In this same year of 1631, the English made an important alteration in the arrangements for their Persian trade. The country round Surat had been ruined by famine and flood, so that the outlook for 1632 was far from promising. In these circumstances, the factors at Surat resolved to concentrate their

[1]*James, William, Blessing, Intelligence, Discovery* and *Reformation.* Gombrun was reached on February 17th and the ships left just over a month later, the first three arriving at Swally on the 15th April.

[2]An account of the fall and recapture of Mombasa will be found on pp. 475-487 of Faria y Sousa's *Asia Portuguesa*, (Lisboa, 1675). The first attempt to retake it was repulsed with heavy loss and the expedition returned defeated to Goa, but the rebels abandoned the place without fighting immediately afterwards, when it was re-occupied by a small force which had been left to blockade it.

efforts on the Persian silk trade, and with this end in view, after the despatch of the usual Persia fleet at the beginning of 1632,[1] they made arrangements to send the outward-bound fleet straight from its usual rendezvous at the Comoro islands to Gombrun, in addition to despatching two vessels for the coast of Coromandel to take in freight goods for Persia. The factors at Gombrun strongly objected to this decision when they heard of it ; one of their reasons being that no transport could be obtained during the hot season when the vessels from England were due to arrive, so that the goods would lie at the port, exposed to capture by Ruy Freyre's frigates. The President and council at Surat, overruled the objections, pointing out that it was in the highest degree unlikely that the Portuguese, who were living in Kung under an agreement made with the Shah, would dare to attempt any robbery at a port of his, and thus expose their own factory to reprisals. They further added that the protection afforded by " Gombroone Castle " might surely be relied on. This reading of the situation was apparently correct, as Ruy Freyre made no attempt to interfere with the ships of his old acquaintance Captain John Weddell, which reached Gombrun in October and left for Surat after a stay in the port of twenty days.[2]

---

[1]*Mary, Exchange, Blessing* and *William* under Captain Slade. They were back at Swally by the middle of April. A Dutch fleet consisting of the *Amboyna, Vlissingen, 't Hoff van Hollandt, 's-Gravenhage, Vere, 't Wapen ven Delft, Buiren* and *Malacca*, under the command of Philips Lucaszoon, was in Gombrun at the same time.

[2]Foster. *English Factories*, 1630-1633, pp. xxv-vi, 140, 195, 235-239. Weddell's fleet consisted of the *Charles, Jonas, Dolphin, Hart* and *Swallow* from England, together with the *Sea-horse, James* and *Intelligence* from Surat, which they had met off the Comoro islands. On reaching Gombrun in October, they found the *Mary* and *Exchange* with freight goods from Masulipatam in the road, as also the Dutch ships *Utrecht, Amboina* and *Grol*, under Jan Carstenszoon from Batavia.

This concentration of English shipping in the Gulf had revived the plans of the Khan of Shiras for the capture of Muscat, on which he was as bent as ever. Both English and Dutch had been broached about the matter, and hitherto both had replied with evasive answers. This time, however, each believed the other to be in earnest, with the result that they both promised to assist the Persian for fear of being forestalled by their rivals. The Khan of Shiras commenced to assemble troops for the expedition in 1632, and he further presented the Hollanders with some of the now rotten and leaky Portuguese frigates taken at Ormuz in 1622, in order that the Dutch might use them for in-shore work against the Portuguese light craft at Kung, Bahrein and elsewhere.[1] Only three Dutch vessels arrived at Gombrun in October, so that the Khan was forced to abandon the idea, as the English likewise displayed no undue eagerness to go. At this point, death removed two of the chief protagonists from the scene, for in December, 1632, Ruy Freyre, who had been in poor health ever since his return from Goa the previous year, died of dysentry at Muscat, worn out by his twelve years continuous active service in the trying climate of the Gulf ; whilst almost at the same time, his old opponent the Imam Quli Khan, the captor of Ormuz, was executed together with most of his family, by his treacherous and ungrateful master Shah Safi.[2] This was the news which Weddell found awaiting him at Gombrun, whither he had sailed from Swally at the beginning of

[1]MacLeod, *Oost-Indische Compagnie als Zeemogendheid in Azie*, 1602-1652, I, p. 450. Foster, *English Factories*, 1630-1633, p. 319. The English informed the Portuguese of this plan early in 1634, during the negotiations for a truce, *Diario do Conde de Linhares*, p. 29.

[2]The best and fullest contemporary accounts of this tragedy are to be found in the documents printed in MacLeod, *Oost-Indische Compagnie*, etc., II, pp. 74-76.

February, 1633, with a fleet of four sail, specially fitted out with the idea of helping the Khan of Shiras to take Muscat. Announcing these tidings in a letter to the Company from Gombrun at the end of March, he wrote, " I had a letter since my being att Gombroone from the [Khan] of Serash concerning the business of Muskatt ; but that designe perished with his death ; and now since the death of Refrera in December [last], who was Governor in Muskatt and hee which formerly burnt your ships and was busie at sea with his frigotts, which are now more quiett, the Dutch gave it out that they will undertake Muskatt for themselves. I will beleeve it when I see it, for without the land forces of the [Khan] it is impossible to be effected." Ruy Freyre had indeed been active to the end, for on December 1st, 1632, the Dutch ships in Gombrun had been alarmed by the news that he was cruising off Larak with a fleet of nearly twenty sail ; although their anxiety was relieved when they heard on the last day of the old year, that Ruy Freyre was dead, and that all his flotilla had retired to Muscat under shelter of the Castle walls.[1]

Deprived of their redoubtable champion, " the mainstay of the soldiery in this India " as a contemporary writer described him, the Portuguese feared more than ever for an attack on Muscat ; for apart

---

[1]*Cf.* Weddell's letter from Gombrun, 24/iii/1633, calendered in Foster, *op. cit.*, p. 295 and Hendrik Hagenaer's *Journal* under 1/xii/1632, and 30/xii/1632, printed in Vol. II of the *Begin ende Voortgangh*, (Amsterdam, 1646). It is quite clear from these and other contemporary sources, that Ruy Freyre died in December 1632, and not in September 1633, as stated in the *Commentaries*. This latter date was accepted both by Sir William Foster (Vol. 1630-1633, p. 295, *n.* 2) and myself (*Commentaries*, p. 210, *note*), but Hagenaer's evidence is quite conclusive as he was at Ormuz at the time. Furthermore, practically all the dates given in the original 1647 edition of the *Commentaries* are demonstrably wrong, and the chronology is hopelessly confused as I have shown elsewhere. Further confirmation is afforded by the entry under February 24th, 1634, of the *Dagh-Register gehouden in't Casteel Batavia.*

from the lack of English or Dutch maritime aid, only the terror of Ruy Freyre's name amongst the inhabitants of the Gulf littoral, had previously prevented the Persian threats from being translated into action. Fortunately, the almost simultaneous removal from the scene of the doughty old Imam Quli Khan, had deprived the Persians of their most trusted leader, whilst neither English nor Dutch made any vigorous attempts to take the matter up with his successors. Furthermore, two at least of the contending parties were no longer enemies, for the Anglo-Portuguese *rapprochment*, which culminated in the agreement of January, 1635, had by now begun.[1] Indirect negotiations between the Viceroy at Goa, and the newly-arrived and energetic head of the English Factory at Surat, William Methwold, had been carried on through the intermediary of the Jesuit Fathers in this latter place and at Damão, all through 1633 ; but it was not until the end of the year that Methwold finally wrote offering to " lay by these our unwilling armes," and to " participate in all mutual offices of assured amity." The Conde de Linhares and his councillors readily closed with the offer, and granted full and ample safe-conducts for the English representatives to proceed to Goa to negotiate a definite peace. This they did in December, 1634, but as early as April, Methwold had issued instructions to Captain Weddell, who was bound for Persia, and to all other commanders, that no Portuguese shipping

[1] The best outline of the course of the negotiations is to be found on pp. xxxv-xxxvii of the 1630-1633 volume of Foster's *English Factories*. On the Portuguese side, the *Diario do Conde de Linhares*, may be consulted with profit for the final stages. Tentative negotiations had been started by the English representatives at Madrid in 1630-1631, but the Council of Portugal, elated with the news of Botelho's victories at Malaca and Sumatra in 1629-1630 scornfully rejected the proposals with the *dictum* that " India had been gained with the sword, and with the sword it would be defended." (*Livros das Monções, Livro* 30, fl. 263.)

was to be attacked. With the promulgation of this order, Anglo-Portuguese rivalry in the Persian Gulf became once and for all a thing of the past—at any rate in so far as armed hostilities were concerned, and even of purely commercial rivalry there was henceforth little or none. Whatever the reactions caused elsewhere, the signing of the definitive agreement at Goa on January 18th, 1635, brought nothing but good to both of the erstwhile enemies in the Gulf ; and the signatories to that memorable document, had every reason to congratulate themselves on thus fortunately terminating a situation which had become " flat, stale and unprofitable " to all concerned.

The story of Anglo-Portuguese rivalry in the Persian Gulf from 1615 to 1635 affords us some interesting examples of the influence of sea-power on history, and of the penalties which follow the loss of the command of the sea, either in whole or in part. Thanks to their complete control of the sea routes in the Gulf, the Portuguese held undisputed sway over all maritime commerce in that region, down to the appearance of the English in force. That this fact was appreciated at Lisbon and at Madrid, is clear from the decision to send a powerful squadron of galleons, under such a picked commander as Ruy Freyre, for the express purpose of nipping the growing English commerce in the bud in 1619. Shilling's victory off Jask in the following year was an important check to the Portuguese, but it did not have the decisive results it might have had, owing to the failure of the English to follow up their success by completely destroying Ruy Freyre's shattered hulks. The result was that the

Portuguese were still as great a menace as ever, and with Ruy Freyre's fleet still in being, they were soon in a position to challenge the English for the supremacy once more. This fact was realised by the experienced old Governor, Fernão de Albuquerque, who, despite the almost total lack of resources against which he had to struggle at Goa, spared no pains to despatch powerful reinforcements to Ruy Freyre, at the same time urging upon him the necessity of giving battle again to the English fleet.

Ruy Freyre's inability or unwillingness to recognise the soundness of this advice, was the real reason of the fall of Ormuz; for his voluntary abandonment of the galleons, in order to carry out the expedition to Kishm, played into the hands of the English and Persians, as the authorities at Goa had foreseen.[1] There was now nothing to prevent the English from proceeding direct to Ormuz, instead of their usual half-way house at Jask, and, after uniting with the Persians, shutting the door of the trap in which Ruy Freyre had placed himself. This once accomplished, the fall of Ormuz was merely a matter of time; for however obstinate the defence, the Castle was bound to fall if not succoured from the sea—and this was rendered impossible by the immolation and destruction of Ruy Freyre's galleons under the Castle walls, since there was no other naval force in Portuguese India capable of giving battle to the English vessels.   Too late Ruy

[1]Compare Fernão d'Albuquerque's letters to Ruy Freyre quoted in note 1 on page 73 *supra*. In justice to Ruy Freyre it should be said that he apparently realised the importance of maintaining an adequate armada to cope with the English, even if he did not put his convictions fully into practice. In a letter written shortly after his defeat at Jask, he wrote " Realms which are situated on the shores of the sea, and which have therein such far-flung fortresses as His Majesty has in this, cannot be preserved without well-equipped fleets ; and if His Majesty does not provide the same, India will be lost, as likewise its strongholds, and this one first of all." (Letter of Ruy Freyre, Ormuz, 12/ii/1621. *British Museum, Egerton MSS.*)

Freyre saw his error, and although, on his escape from captivity, he was anxious to make a last desperate attempt to retrieve the situation, by surprising the victorious Anglo-Persian forces in the middle of their plundering orgies, the irresolution of his companion, Constantino de Sa, lost him this last chance. It was a slender one at best, for even assuming the bold stroke had succeeded (which was after all quite possible), the fortress could never have been made tenable for long against a renewed Anglo-Persian attack, since Ruy Freyre had no galleons wherewith to oppose the English ships, which were the decisive factor in the situation, as they assured the passage of the Persian troops from the mainland.

It must be admitted that Ruy Freyre, if he was mainly to blame for the fall of Ormuz, owing to his neglect to dispute the command of the sea with the English in 1621-1622, subsequently made amends as far as it lay within his power to do so. Although provided with only slender forces and indifferent troops, he broke up the threatened Persian attack on Muscat, reconquered much of the lost ground on the Arabian coast, and blockaded Ormuz so closely that it twice came within an ace of falling into his grasp. Both times however the Persians were relieved by the opportune appearance of the English fleet, against which Ruy Freyre's oared frigates were powerless, except under certain exceptional conditions. The most he could achieve was the rather melancholy satisfaction that even if the Portuguese could not regain Ormuz, its possession proved but a barren and profitless acquisition for the Persians.

The appearance of Botelho's armada in 1625, seemed to afford another hope of reversing the situation but this was not really so. It is true that the masterly way in which Botelho handled his squadron and sought to give battle to his enemies under all and every conditions, caused the English no little worry and annoyance, but there was no corresponding lasting advantage for the Portuguese. The appearance of the Hollanders on the scene in 1623, introduced yet another complication from the Lusitanian point of view, since the two heretic nations made common cause together. The indomitable behaviour of Ruy Freyre and Botelho, did indeed hearten their men to such an extent that the Portuguese regained much of the prestige they had lost; whilst the English and Dutch were forced to navigate together for mutual protection, often with unduly large and costly fleets. The annual cruise to the Comoro islands by the English, in order to protect their outward-bound shipping from being waylaid by the Portuguese galleons, was also an expensive waste of time, but the Portuguese could never establish a decided superiority over the allied forces, which were increasing yearly, whilst their own decreased as rapidly. Furthermore, even if Botelho and Ruy Freyre had succeeded in regaining Ormuz, the place was by now little better than a heap of ruins, its erstwhile trade having been diverted to Muscat, Basra and Gombrun; whilst it is very unlikely that the Portuguese could have held it against the overwhelming forces the allies could have brought to bear against them.

Nevertheless, the advantage was not wholly on the side of English and Persians. The European ships were only present at Gombrun for a month or two in the year, and for the rest of the season the whole littoral on the Persian side lay exposed to the ravages of Ruy Freyre's waspish flotillas, which had unchallenged control of the Gulf from Cape Ras Musandam to the Shatt el Arab. It was entirely owing to the presence of Portuguese galliots in the Euphrates, that the

Persians were foiled in their efforts to take Basra in 1624-1625, although otherwise the place would have fallen into their hands like a rotten apple after the capture of Baghdad from the Turks. Indeed so paralysing was the effect of the pressure exercised by Ruy Freyre on coast-wise commerce in the Gulf, that the Persians, despairing of effective aid from their European friends, were compelled to give the Portuguese a settlement at Kung, on the same terms as they had granted their victorious English allies a factory at Gombrun eight years earlier. All this was due to the cardinal error of their not following up the capture of Ormuz in 1622 by an immediate attack on Muscat, which would then have fallen in all probability. As it was, Ruy Freyre made such use of the breathing space afforded, that he was able to carry the war into the enemy's camp with a vengeance. A brave man struggling with adversity is always an exhilarating sight, but Ruy Freyre and Nuno Alvarez Botelho were more than that. They were bonny fighters worthy of any man's steel; and it was indeed fortunate for England that she was represented in the Gulf at this time by men of the stamp of John Weddell and Edward Monnox, who well and truly laid the foundations of that supremacy which has lasted down to the present day.

APPENDIX.

The following brief descriptions of some Portuguese factories or agencies in the Gulf during the period under review, are based on the accounts of them contained in Antonio Bocarro's *Livro do Estado da India Oriental*, written at Goa during the year 1634.

Only a few of the more obscure places have been selected, as voluminous accounts of the more celebrated ones, such as Ormuz, Muscat and Gombrun, are readily available in print in the works of Linschoten, Pedro Teixeira, Pietro della Valle, Olearius and other travellers, too numerous to mention here.

BASRA (Bassora).

Although the Portuguese frequented this place to some extent during the sixteenth century, they did not resort there in large numbers until after the fall of Ormuz, when Ruy Freyre tried to make it the chief entrepôt for the Gulf, as a counterpoise to Gombrun. Basra was at this time governed by a Pasha who owed a nominal allegiance to the Turkish government, but who was to all intents and purposes independent. After the capture of Baghdad, the Pasha was hard pressed by the Persians, but this pressure was relieved by the despatch of Dom Gonçalo da Silveira's galliots in 1624, which effectually checked the Persian invasion, as narrated in the text. Navigation from Muscat to Basra was carried out in all seasons of the year by coasting along the Persian littoral and making use of the prevailing winds. The city was well fortified, and Bocarro estimates the total population at some 15,000, in addition to the large Beduin encampments in the neighbourhood. The Portuguese *cafila* or convoy of merchant ships, that went from Muscat to Basra each year, was usually escorted by only one man-of-war, as the English and Dutch vessels did not come higher up the Gulf than Gombrun, whilst the Portuguese galliots were considered to be more than a match for such Nakhilu (Niquilla) pirates as might venture to attack them. For their commercial voyages in the Gulf, the Portuguese used chiefly small craft such as *fustas* or foists, *terradas*, *terranquins*, galliots, frigates and the like.[1] Their cargoes consisted mainly of such goods as they had formerly imported into Persia *via* Ormuz, of which spices and fine cloths yielded the greatest profits. The most profitable investment in return was pearls, but many European goods could be secured, which came on camel caravan overland from Aleppo. Bocarro estimates that nearly 500,000 *xerafines* were invested annually in this trade, though the profits varied considerably. He gives a very unflattering description of the inhabitants (in which he is borne out by most other contemporary writers), stigmatizing them as being " very fat, white, weak and cowardly " and " much addicted to sodomy despite the unusual beauty of their women." He admits nevertheless that the Portuguese were exceedingly well treated by the local authorities, and that the Pasha kept faith with with them very well, save on some occasions when he was justly provoked by their own wanton misdeeds.[2] He speaks very highly of the excellent wine, grapes and fruits to be had, and particularly commends the marmalade and dates. The Portuguese had two churches in Basra, one of the bare-footed Carmelites, and the other belonging to the Augustinians, whose congregations included many Armenian and Assyrian Christians, of whose rites he gives an account. Della Valle, who was at Basra in 1625, has left us a not very edifying description of the behaviour of the Reverend Fathers towards each other. It is interesting to note that Bocarro speaks very highly of the martial qualities of the Assyrian Christians, and states that the Conde de Linhares encouraged them to emigrate to Muscat, Ceylon and other Portuguese settlements, where their fighting value would be welcome—an anticipation of our own Assyrian levies raised in 1918.

QATIF (Catifa).

The importance of Qatif as a centre of Portuguese trade in the Gulf, likewise dates from the loss of Ormuz. The district was under the rule of an Arab Sheikh, who, like the Pasha of Basra, acknowledged a shadowy vassalage to the Ottoman Sultans. The Sheikh, or Pasha

[1]For detailed descriptions of these types of sailing vessels, see Dalgado, *Glossario Luso-Asiatico*, (Coimbra, 1919-1921).

[2]The terms on which the Portuguese were established at Basra, are to be found on pp. 271-272 of Vol. II of the *Chronista de Tissuary*, (Nova Goa, 1867). Della Valle also gives a summary of them. The prosperity of the Portuguese factory received its first check with the appearance of the English in 1640, who were followed by the Dutch six years later. The factory then declined and was given up for some years, but was re-established in 1695. In Bocarro's time, the Pasha was named Ali.

as he was called by the Portuguese, was at more or less open enmity with the Persians of Bahrein, and hence the alliance with the Portuguese, and the support he received from Ruy Freyre in 1627. All the local trade was in the hands of the Pasha or his sons, whose monopoly had anything but a beneficial effect on commerce in general. Nevertheless, the place was important on account of the fact that it yielded the finest Arabian horses which could be had for money ; and great profits were realised on the sale of these in India. The most expensive of them did not cost more than 200 *patacas*,[1] whilst some could be had for as little as 50 or 60. They were brought down to Qatif from the interior by the Beduins. There were also great quantities of seed-pearls from the Bahrein beds to be obtained at Qatif, since most of the pearl-fishers came from this latter district. These horses and pearls were paid for by the Portuguese, with cloths and linen from Sind and Cambay, and with silver money in the form of *larins* and *abexins*. A subsidiary export was that of dates, which although not so fine as those of Basra, made a better and more lasting product when dried. Bocarro gives an interesting description of the Beduins' marriage ceremonies, which included betrothal by capture. The exact amount of money invested in the Qatif horse trade is not stated, but he admits that it amounted to many thousands of *cruzados* or ducats, a year.

KUNG (Congo).

The Portuguese factory at Kung was founded by Ruy Freyre in 1630 under the circumstances related in the text. In accordance with the agreement made at that time with the Khan of Shiras, the Portuguese were to enjoy a moiety of all Customs dues levied on goods entering the port, in the same way as the English did at Gombrun, but in both cases considerable difficulty was experienced in extracting the amounts claimed from the Persians. Despite the continual threat of a Persian attack on Muscat, and the intermittent state of war in the Gulf which continued even after the negotiation of the truce in 1630, the Portuguese factory at Kung remained unmolested by the Persians, and even attained quite a considerable prosperity. In 1633 there was some talk of transferring it to a site three miles from Gombrun, which would have had a bad effect on

---

[1]*Pataca* in Portuguese, or *Patacoon* in English, was the old Indo-European name for the dollar or piece-of-eight. *Larin* was Persian bar silver money, of which 5 *Larins* were worth one *pataca*. The *Abexin* (also written *Abassi*, *Abassee*, etc.) was a kind of Persian silver money, first coined by Shah Abbas II (whence the name) about 1600 and worth some 300 Portuguese *reis*, or sixteen pence of English money according to Herbert and Fryer.

the English receipts from the Gombrun customs, as the Hollanders noted with malicious satisfaction. The proposal never materialised, however, and perhaps was never seriously intended ; although the local Persian Governor was anxious to make a definite peace with the Portuguese, whereby the coast would be free from the raids of their flotillas the whole year round, and not merely for six months, as had been stipulated by Ruy Freyre.[1]

The chief importance of Kung to the Portuguese lay in the revenue derived from the neighbouring pearl fisheries.

The roadstead of Kung was an open one, and only protected to a slight extent against northerly, north-east and north-west winds, but small ships could anchor within a musket-shot of the shore. The chief imports from Muscat were cloths and other goods from Cambay, Sind and district, indigo, spices, raw hides and gold. The exports included Persian goods of all sorts, such as silks, carpets and rose-water, which were brought down on camels from the interior. In addition, a good amount of silver bullion was obtained in the form of *Abbasis* and *Larins*. The export of horses was forbidden by the Shah under pain of death, but it was usually possible to obtain some. The town, though composed of well-built stone and adobe houses, was only a small one with a resident population of some two hundred Persians, Parsees and Arabs, but there were often large encampments of these latter in the neighbourhood. On account of Ruy Freyre's destructive activities, the Portuguese were held in great respect by the Persians, save that they had always to be prepared to encounter opposition at sea from the Nakhilau (Niquilla) pirates who were described as being a race of hardy free-booters. A similar pirate clan, the Nautaques, had given the Portuguese much trouble in the past, but had been practically exterminated as a result of Ruy Freyre's punitive expeditions.

DOBBAH (Doba).

The Portuguese fort at Dobbah was a small but strongly constructed work, which served to dominate the neighbouring walled town of the same name, whose population of about one thousand Arabs included but few men at arms. Date-palms and seed-pearls formed the principal product of the neighbouring land and sea respectively, but the gathering of both was frequently impeded by the raids of the local Imam. This fortress, together with the others on the Arabian coast (except Muscat and Sohar),

[1]*Dagh-Register Batavia*, 1634, pp. 261, 338. *Diario do Conde de Linhares*, 1634, pp. 9-10.

had been built by Ruy Freyre, and garrisoned by him on behalf of the titular King of Ormuz, whose son served for some time in Ruy Freyre's armadas. They were used as provisioning depots for the fleets, and for ports of refuge in case of necessity, but their value as such was substantially decreased when the new Imam opened hostilities against the Portuguese after the death of Ruy Freyre.

KHOR FAKKAN (Corfocam).

The small triangular Portuguese fort at this place was constructed by Gaspar Leite in 1620. It was garrisoned only by a small detachment of Lascarins, or Arab auxiliaries, under a captain of the same nationality. Its only importance lay in the fact that it was the first harbour north of Muscat, with a safe anchorage in all winds for vessels up to three or four hundred tons, whilst the local wells produced the best drinking water in all Arabia.

SOHAR (Soar).

The small, but strongly-built fortress of Sohar was garrisoned by a detachment of forty Portuguese soldiers under a captain, supported by some hundred and fifty Lascarins. There was an Augustinian church within the walls, and a Customs-house on the shore, which yielded an annual income of over 200 " *pardaus* of larins." The chief products were date-palms and the seed-pearl fisheries along the coast, but the cultivation of the former was frequently impeded by hostilities with the local inhabitants. There was also a great deal of game to be shot in the neighbourhood, and a plentiful supply of birds which were hawked with falcons. On the site of the old ruined city, a large number of Roman gold coins of Tiberius Cæsar had been dug up in the year 1601, which afforded proof that the place had been of considerable importance in Roman times.

CHAPTER IV.

The Treaties of 1642, 1654 and 1661.

On December 1st, 1640, a group of nobles in Lisbon, with the support of the people, overthrew the government of Philip IV and terminated the union of Portugal and Spain, which had lasted for sixty years. Some days afterwards, John, Duke of Braganza, a descendant of the ancient sovereigns, was formally acclaimed King under the title of John IV, and when the news of the Restoration reached them, the colonies gladly adhered to the new regime.

In 1580 the overseas possessions of Portugal had been numerous and some of them extensive, but they were scattered over three continents and many seas. In Africa they included fortresses in Morocco, an infant colony in Angola on the west coast and an older one in Mozambique on the east ; in Asia, fortresses and settlements in Arabia, Persia, India, Indonesia and China ; in America, Brazil. In addition, three groups of Atlantic islands displayed the banner of the Quinas. The widespread nature of this dominion exposed it to successful attack when Portugal accepted the rule of Philip II and the enemies of Spain became also hers, so that John IV took up an inheritance which had considerably diminished between 1580 and 1640. The principal aggressors were the Dutch East and West India Companies.

The former expelled the Portuguese from the Moluccas, began the conquest of Ceylon and, on the eve of the Restoration, captured Malacca, the key of the narrow strait by which the most valuable products of the Far East reached the West. The State of India as it was called, which stretched from East Africa to China, was thus deprived of its strongest outposts, and nearly all its trade, since Ormuz had fallen to an Anglo-Persian force in 1622 and the very city of Goa, the capital, once called the Golden, found itself blockaded by a Dutch fleet.

The commercial losses were more important than the territorial, for the Dutch by these acquisitions went far towards gaining a monopoly of the trade in drugs and spices which the Portuguese had wrested from the Arabs and enjoyed for more than a century.

On the other side of the globe the West India Company overran a large part of the Brazilian littoral, inspired by the same commercial aims, but in this case sugar was the principal lure. In 1630 Pernambuco fell into its hands and became the capital and some years later five of the captaincies into which Brazil had been divided recognised the authority of the Company. With the advent of Count Maurice of Nassau, a farseeing statesman as well as a distinguished soldier, the Dutch seemed likely to master the whole country and this might have happened if the Directors at home had followed his advice, for in 1640 all Brazil north of the River S. Francisco, except Maranham, which was acquired in the following year, and Sergipe to the south of it, belonged to the Company. At the same time its fleet rivalled in numbers those of Spain and Portugal combined and disputed the command of the South Atlantic with the former owners ; as early as 1626 the

Company could put 84 warships on the sea and from 1623 to 1638 captured no fewer than 540 Spanish and Portuguese vessels.

These enormous losses, which hurt their pride and emptied their pockets, were attributed by the Portuguese to the Spanish connection and more than anything else rendered it odious to them. They remembered that they had formerly been on friendly terms with the Dutch and that King Sebastian had even encouraged the latter in their revolt against Philip II. Indeed, until 1580, Portugal had never been involved in war with a European power, save with Spain, and during the previous hundred years she had lived in cordial relations with her neighbour, based on the blood relationship between the respective sovereigns.

Her geographical position at the extreme south west of the Continent removed her from international complications and in the interest of their country Kings Manuel I, John III, and Sebastian consistently maintained a policy of neutrality. This policy was wise and even necessary for a small nation with far-flung colonies and a trading monopoly to defend, and it was adhered to in the face of the continuous attacks of French and English corsairs on the Portuguese merchantmen and on Brazilian territory.

Between 1580 and 1640, however, the political situation and the balance of power in Europe suffered a profound and permanent alteration, with the rise of England, Holland and France and the decline of Spain, and when John IV ascended the throne, he not only found himself at war with the Dutch in Asia and America, but *ipso facto* exposed himself to a life and death struggle with the neighbouring nation. Though he made a truce for ten years with Holland in 1641, it was ill-observed and a definite peace did not come until 1669. In the intervening years the Portuguese were driven from Ceylon and from the fortresses of Cochin and Cananor, they lost and regained Angola, and they recovered the Dutch conquests in Brazil. The war with Spain dragged on until 1668 and, though every pitched battle ended in a Portuguese victory, all save one were fought on Portuguese soil and the help of French and English soldiers and of English diplomats was needed before Spain would admit defeat, agree to what she considered her dismemberment, and recognise the new dynasty of Braganza.

This successful issue was often in doubt, and John IV entered upon his reign with some obvious military handicaps as well as an empty treasury. Although in decline, Spain was still a great power; the frontier fortresses had not been kept in repair, two thousand cannon had been removed, the few regiments of regular Portuguese troops were stationed in Flanders, and a separate navy did not exist, but the King could rely on the patriotism of his people, on the internal troubles of Spain and on promises of French aid. The Catalonian revolt, supported by France, prevented the Spanish government from attempting an invasion of Portugal for many years, and Richelieu was glad of the opportunity to put his enemy between two fires. He refused to make the formal league which the ambassadors of John IV asked for and had reason to expect, because he wished to be free to make peace with Spain when it suited him, but his recognition of her independence was of great value to Portugal ; French officers and men strengthened the Portuguese army, French ships secured the coast from attack and it was under French auspices that representatives of Portugal were able to attend the Congress of Munster. The Dutch, who were allies of France in the Thirty Years War, then in progress, welcomed the Revolution of 1640, in the hope

133

that it would weaken Spain, but soon found that the revival of Portugal conflicted with their interests, for John IV declined to make more than a truce with them, because he hoped to recover the colonies which had been lost in the time of the Philips.

The Anglo-Portuguese alliance dating from 1373 had fallen into abeyance after 1580, and in view of the amicable relations subsisting between England and Spain, John IV could not expect military assistance from the former power, but he relied on obtaining her recognition of his title and neutrality in his conflict with the latter in exchange for freedom of trade for Englishmen in Portugal. His ambassadors who started for London in February, 1641, were instructed to ask for these and also for confirmation of the truce in India which had been made between the Portuguese viceroy and the President of the East India Company in 1635.

The personnel of the embassy was carefully chosen ; D. Antão de Almada had a title in his family—that of Count of Avranches—which had been conferred by Henry VI, Andrade Leitão belonged to the judiciary, as did the secretary, Sousa de Macedo, and the last earned the friendship of Charles I and published in London a learned work setting forth his master's rights to the throne, entitled *Lusitania Liberata.* Though their request for admission was opposed by the Spanish ambassador, it was granted because they offered "liberty of religion and other fair conditions to the English merchants." At their private audience in April, 1641, the King expressed his desire to renew the traditional friendship with Portugal and advised that the fortification of the frontiers should be attended to, while the Queen " did them much honour," because she was the sister of Louis XIII and knew the welcome their colleagues had received in France.

The nobility followed the example of their sovereigns,

and members of other classes manifested a like friendliness, but from self-interest rather than from love for Portugal. The Spaniards were unpopular, and many Englishmen, since the Reformation had altered the national mentality, felt, as they still feel, a sympathy for foreign revolutionaries ; in this case it was more deserved than it has usually been.

Commissioners were appointed to treat with the ambassadors and we have a record from the Portuguese side of the conferences between them, but as they are not always dated, the sequence of events is far from clear. The general articles of mutual amity and trade in the European dominions of each power were easily arranged, but in June an event occurred which had the effect of greatly prolonging the negotiations. The Portuguese still clung to the trading monopoly with their colonies, but they had been obliged to relax it in part ; after the truce of 1635 they had given permission to English vessels to trade to their settlements on the coast of India and Macau, and now, to obtain a truce with Holland, the Portuguese ambassador Mendonça Furtado made far wider concessions by the treaty which he signed with the States General on June 12th. On hearing this, the English commissioners asked that these concessions should be extended to their countrymen, and the demand caused the ambassadors considerable embarassment and led to months of discussion in London and Lisbon.

The articles of the treaty of June 12th specially debated were the 17th, 20th, and 24th. By article 17 it was stipulated that if the Portuguese needed foreign ships for their Brazil trade, they should be bound to buy or hire them in Holland. The English had traded clandestinely to Brazil for a century and now sought to do so openly and directly, but all they could obtain was that the employment of English ships should be referred to two commissioners to settle. In the event, however, it was an outside circumstance and not the latter who solved the problem. The relations of Portugal with Holland soon became so strained that she had no desire to employ Dutch vessels, and English took their place.

Article 20 provided for free trade between the Portuguese and Dutch settlements on the West African coast and the island of S. Thomas in the Gulf of Guinea in slaves, gold and merchandise and the English commissioners claimed a similar concession, but the ambassadors objected with reason that the cases were not parallel, because the English had no settlement in those parts to which the Portuguese could resort. Their one factory on the Gambia had small importance and was not even mentioned in the discussions, so far as we know. However, as the Portuguese had already opened the door to the Dutch, there was little advantage in closing it to the English, and as Portugal needed all the friends she could purchase, a compromise was effected. English merchants established in Africa were to be allowed to carry on business as hitherto, and commissioners appointed for the purpose were to arrange a free commerce.

Article 24 gave the Dutch liberty of conscience and worship, while the instructions given by John IV to his ambassadors only allowed them to consent to a clause similar to that contained in the treaty of November 15th, 1630, between England and Spain. The commissioners asked that English merchants should not be subject to the Inquisition and claimed the same rights as those just conceded to the subjects of the United Provinces, and the point was referred to Lisbon. By decree of September 22nd, John IV committed its examination to a *junta* of theologians presided over by the Archbishop of Lisbon, which decided against the leave for freedom of worship granted by the treaty of June 12th, even in private houses, because it was only lawful for Christian princes to act negatively in this matter, and not to give positive permission. The *junta* therefore proposed that the precedent of 1630, securing non-Catholics from molestation on account of their religious views and practices should be followed, although they saw no objection to its being stated that the English would be treated in the same way as the subjects of other princes. The compromise was accepted by the commissioners and incorporated in Article 19 of the Anglo-Portuguese treaty. This was finally signed on January 29th, 1642, and re-established in part the secular alliance which still continues and is the oldest existing between any two states. The ambassadors left London soon afterwards and the secretary remained as resident. He had already shown his ability as a controversialist with Spaniards, henceforth for some years his struggles were to be with Englishmen.

In the diplomatic sphere he had little business to transact because of the Civil War, but he played a minor part in English domestic affairs.

For religious and personal reasons, the sympathies of John IV were entirely with Charles I in the struggle with his rebellious subjects and Sousa de Macedo, who shared his master's views, arranged for gratuitous supplies of arms and ammunition to the King ; he was the safest and finally the only intermediary of Charles's correspondence with his supporters and with the Queen, when she retired to Holland and afterwards to France, and as a reward for his services, Charles II on ascending the throne, gave his son the title of Lord Mullingar. Sousa de Macedo deserved this mark of favour, because he had taken considerable risks and suffered many vexations at the hands of the Parliamentarians; when the King's cabinet was captured at the battle of Naseby in June, 1645, the resident's relations with Charles became manifest and he was violently attacked in the House of Commons, not only for having facilitated the Royal correspondence, but also for his negotiations for the marriage of the future Charles II to a Portuguese Infanta.

In July his post from France was stopped and handed over to a committee whose duty it was to examine letters, and he was summoned to be present at their opening, but he had foreseen this step and played a trick on the examiners; the bundle was found to contain old newspapers and three sealed letters. These they opened eagerly, but only found crosses, comic characters and the picture of a man handing spectacles to the committee to read the letters. The incident leaked out and caused much amusement in the town, and the resident continued to transmit the Royal correspondence. He knew the importance to England of trade with his country, and though Parliament decided to ask John IV to recall him, he would not allow himself to be intimidated. When in August his letters were again held up, he threatened reprisals against English goods in Portugal and on the representations of the merchants trading to that country, the letters were restored intact. In June, 1643, he had used a similar threat with equal success when a band of soldiers sought to enter and search the embassy for conspirators; it was situate in Lincoln's Inn Fields, hence the name Portugal Street, which now runs at the back of the square. Shortly after this, a committee of the Commons waited on him to protest against the resort of Catholics to his house to hear Mass, but he insisted on his privilege. The martyrdom of priests, which he witnessed, excited his ire against the Puritans, and his action in sending out a chaplain to Father Hugh Macmahon when on the way to execution was referred to the Committee of Both Kingdoms. Whenever the interests of Portugal and religion were concerned, he acted as boldly as if he represented a great power and not a small and poor country struggling to maintain its independence.

Apart from differences with Parliament, Sousa de Macedo, complained in his letters of the disturbed state of England and the climate; except when he went to Oxford to see the King, he dared not leave London, nor even go far from the embassy, lest it should be assaulted on the ground that goods belonging to Catholics were deposited there. These fears were shared by the Spanish ambassador, while de Sabran, the French ambassador, who had married an English-woman, was constantly insulted by the populace.

As to the climate, Sousa de Macedo remarked : " for five years I have not seen the sun as God made it ; I have spent five winters in which the days are bright nights, and five summers in which the days are dark; in the winters I am always trembling with cold and in the summer with pest ; the men I meet are at least half drunk, and my only recreation has been the hope of getting back to Portugal." This letter is dated January 25th, 1646 and soon afterwards he had his desire. Before leaving England he prepared a manifesto to Parliament, denying that he had infringed neutrality and even setting out the favours he considered he had done to it, but his defence is not convincing ; however, the Royalist sympathies of John IV did not carry him so far as the King of Spain, who seized the ships and goods of Parliamentarians and forbade trading to Englishmen who had no passport from Charles.

On the retirement of Sousa de Macedo, his place

was not filled, and Portugal remained for five years without diplomatic representation in London. In 1646, Sir Henry Compton was accredited by Charles I to the Court of Lisbon, but he was recalled in 1648 on the ground that he had hardly anything to do. According to the French envoy, Lanier, he could not get on with his secretary, nor with the English factory, which was divided into two parties, some sympathising with Charles, others with Parliament. The judicial murder of the King on January 30th, 1649, and the arrival of Princes Rupert and Maurice in the Tagus on November 30th with ships of the Royal Navy and prizes, augmented the dissensions of the English colony, and the latter event proved very embarrassing to the Portuguese government and led to a conflict between it and the Commonwealth.

Lisle, envoy of the Princes, had previously been informed that both Royalist and Parliamentarian vessels would be allowed to use the port of Lisbon, but the government was determined to maintain neutrality in the English Civil war and laid down conditions to prevent a conflict in Portuguese waters. The Princes accepted these conditions and were courteously received by John IV, but they did not correspond to the hospitality extended to them. During some months they made Lisbon a basis of operations against the enemy, captured its ships, sold them as prizes and finally ignored the protests made by the Portuguese Secretary of State and the warnings that the Parliamentarians were preparing a fleet to send in pursuit of them. On March 19th, 1650, this arrived at Cascaes under the command of Blake, carrying Charles Vane, who had been ordered to remonstrate with the Portuguese government for its reception of Rupert, and ask for the surrender of his ships and prizes, and when John IV refused the demand, Blake sought to force his way into the Tagus. As the forts proved too strong, Vane urged the King either to let him pass to attack the Princes, or else to compel them to leave. These further demands were considered by the Council of State and, largely owing to a spirited discourse by the heir to the throne, Prince Theodosius, they were rejected; whereupon Blake began hostilities by capturing some ships of the Brazil fleet as it left the river on May 16th. These happened to be the property of English merchants and as a reprisal, some English residents of the Parliamentary faction were arrested and Vane left for home. At the same time the government made further endeavours to get rid of its unwelcome guests, but when Popham came with a second fleet and orders to commence hostilities, Blake instituted a blockade of the river and the Princes found themselves shut in and were unable to leave until the approach of winter drove the English away. In the meantime, John IV had been obliged to take measures to break the blockade and in the course of these the Portuguese and Royalists fleets fought several indecisive actions with those of the Parliament outside the bar, while fourteen vessels of the incoming Brazil fleet fell into Blake's hands.

By their abuse of hospitality the Princes had inflicted a grave injury on their host and, when they departed, John hastened to seek peace with the *de facto* government of England, for he could not afford to be at war with her as well as with Spain and Holland. Moreover, the interests of Portugal and England were not divergent, and he feared the formation of an Anglo-Spanish alliance, seeing that Philip IV had allowed Blake to use Spanish ports in the late conflict and had recognised the Commonwealth. Sousa de Macedo, who was then ambassador in Holland, had begun negotiations with the Parliament for a treaty, and Dr.

John de Guimarães, a lawyer, was sent to London at the end of the year to conclude it and obtain release of the ships and goods taken by Blake.

The new envoy received a poor welcome, and during his two years stay had to struggle with almost insuperable difficulties, among these being the ever changing political situation and foreign enemies. The House of Commons only voted for his admission by a slender majority and though the French ambassador supported him, the Dutch and Spanish ambassadors put every obstacle in his path. The latter, D. Alonso de Cardenas, was a formidable opponent. He had lived long in London, he knew the ways of the country, he possessed many friends, and his government furnished him liberally with money for bribes. Guimarães soon found it necessary to ask for more funds for this purpose. He had been instructed to negotiate a peace treaty, but the Council of State, with whom he treated, would not discuss one until he had agreed to six Preliminary Articles to the following effect :—

(1) the liberation of the Englishmen who had been imprisoned,

(2) restoration of English ships and goods seized, with pecuniary reparation to their owners,

(3) the punishment of those accused of murdering some men who had gone on shore from the Parliamentary fleet and of others who had tried to burn Blake's flagship,

(4) payment of the cost of maintaining the English fleets on the Portuguese coast,

(5) reparation for the goods seized by the Princes, and

(6) restoration of the ships taken by Rupert to Portugal with damages for their detention.

When the first two Articles had been carried into effect and security given for the performance of the other four demands, the Council expressed willingness to grant a truce for six months, during which a peace could be negotiated. This was early in April, 1651, and in May, after long discussions, Guimarães accepted the demands, but made it a condition that the merchants who were to be liberated and to whom restitution was to be made should agree to surrender their persons and goods to King John IV, in case peace was not made within a fixed time. When this offer was refused, he decided to go home to try and persuade the King to accept the English terms, as his instructions did not allow him to go further, whereupon Parliament let him go and resolved that it was not bound by what had passed and that a bill should be prepared for making prizes of Portuguese ships and goods. The demands presented to Guimarães were extraordinary in one respect; reparation was demanded, not as the price of peace, but as the price of beginning negotiations at all, and the envoy could not discover what further demands would be advanced when he had acceded to the six Articles. Moreover, though it seemed reasonable that the losses and damages on both sides should be set off one against the other, the English government insisted on unilateral restitution and was carrying on hostilities against Portugal while in negotiation with her.

Guimarães did not return, but was succeeded by the Count de Penaguião who was given the rank of Ambassador. The former's mission had failed because England refused to continue negotiations until the imprisoned merchants had been released and their goods returned without conditions. John IV found it necessary to yield, and Penaguião, who arrived in September, 1652, was able to say that the English in

Portugal enjoyed their liberty, property and privileges, including freedom from taxation and that their ships and goods had been restored. He came therefore prepared to sign the six Preliminary Articles and this was effected on December 29th. Negotiations then commenced between him and the English merchants in respect of their claims under the Articles, and between him and the commissioners for a treaty. All he desired was the confirmation of the treaty of 1642 ; he had no instructions to ask for new conditions and contended that Parliament should not demand any from him, but the commissioners, backed by the merchants who sent in a list of 38 concessions they wished, had very different views, and sought to profit by Portugal's embarassments. After presenting their demands they added nine additional Articles, the most important of which were the right of pre-emption in respect of the salt exported from Portugal for ten years and the right of entry for English war-ships into Portuguese harbours to revictual and repair. The first point was waived by the new Council of State appointed in May, 1653, after Cromwell had ejected the members from the House of Commons and closed the Long Parliament, the second was insisted upon and incorporated in the treaty. The draft of this, as prepared by the commissioners, contained concessions going far beyond those of 1642, such as the right to trade with all the Portuguese colonies, and this was only agreed to by the ambassador after a long struggle ; in the case of Brazil four kinds of merchandise, which fell within the exclusive rights of the Chartered Company, were excepted.

The commissioners also asked for a large extension of the privileges of the English in Portugal by which they could only be arrested by written permission of the English Judge Conservator, except when *in flagrante delicto* in a criminal case ; they also were to be exempt from any new taxes which might be imposed; when they died, the Portuguese courts were to have no jurisdiction over their property and the goods of their debtors were not to be retained against them by the Inquisition. The religious toleration offered did not satisfy the commissioners ; the English must be permitted to hold Protestant services in their houses, and on board ship, and a site for a cemetery must be assigned to them. The commissioners required yet more. The customs dues were never to exceed twenty-three per cent., nor were they to be altered without leave of the merchants—an arrogant claim which reduced the authority of the King of Portugal in his own dominions. The cumulative effect of all this was to put Englishmen in Portugal in a stronger position than natives of the country.

The Ambassador did his best to get these hard terms mitigated, but in vain, and for the sake of peace he finally bowed to them, while protesting that they exceeded his instructions. Though these have not come down to us, the difficulty made by John IV in ratifying the treaty is evidence that he spoke the truth.

Penaguião had conceded almost everything asked for and had orders to return home; a ship was prepared for him and waited months for the purpose, but he could not get the final draft of the treaty approved ; moreover, fresh difficulties arose which detained him for another year in London. The first payment under the fourth of the Articles was not forthcoming and at the beginning of December occurred the incident at the New Exchange in London which led to his brother's death. D. Pantaleão de Sá, having been (as he thought) insulted by an officer named Gerard, returned there with armed retainers and in the affray which followed, one Greenway was killed in mistake for

Gerard and others were wounded. The populace besieged the Portuguese embassy and Cromwell sent troops and demanded the surrender of D. Pantaleão and his alleged accomplices. The ambassador gave them up, but pleaded privilege for his brother, without avail. The trial was held in due course, and D. Pantaleão and some of his servants were condemned to death. The Spanish and French ambassadors endeavoured to save the former, but Cromwell, who had become Protector, decided that though he was a mere youth D. Pantaleão should die, and he was executed on Tower Hill on July 20th, 1654. A king would probably have shown clemency, but a middle-class usurper could not resist showing his power and satisfying his Puritan supporters by enforcing the last penalty against a man who in their eyes had three things to his disadvantage—he was a Catholic, a noble and a foreigner. In the hope of saving his brother, Penaguião signed the treaty on the eve of the execution and left England in August.

The treaty of 1654 was a diplomatic triumph for the Commonwealth, not only because under its provisions great commercial and religious advantages were secured from Portugal, but also because these had been sought for from Spain and refused ; in return the Portuguese obtained only what concerned peace and mutual friendship. They had to pay dearly for the hospitality to the Princes, but eight years later, after further sacrifices, their services to the House of Stuart were rewarded.

John IV delayed ratification of the treaty owing to the clauses dealing with religious liberty. The Holy See had not recognised his title, owing to Spanish opposition, and he was afraid that if he assented to these clauses, his chance of securing recognition would be further prejudiced. This argument was put before

Cromwell, but did not move him and, under the threat of hostilities delivered by Philip Meadowe, Latin Secretary to the Council of State, who came to the Tagus on Blake's fleet, the King yielded. His death in 1657 and the accession of his youthful son, Alfonso, under the regency of a woman, John's widow, encouraged the Spaniards to make active efforts for the reconquest of Portugal, and Francisco de Mello, afterwards Marquis de Sande, was hastily dispatched to London to try and get his country included in a league against Spain, or in the alternative to obtain military help. The treaty of April 18th, 1660, gave leave to enlist troops for service in Portugal, but, owing to the Restoration, it was not ratified. Nevertheless, Mello found a better way by a marriage between Catherine, Alfonso's sister and Charles II and he offered a dowry of two million *cruzados,* the cession of Tangier and Bombay and permission for the English to trade with all the Portuguese colonies. In return he asked for freedom of worship for Catherine and protection for Portugal against Spain and Holland. The negotiations lasted a year and their successful issue remained in doubt almost to the last moment, owing to the fierce opposition made by Spain and her allies, reinforced by spectacular counter-offers, and lavish bribes and finally by a threat of war. The blustering conduct of the Spanish ambassador Batteville nettled Charles, while the London merchants favoured the Portuguese match because of the advantages offered, but it was the personal intervention of Louis XIV that probably decided English policy in the matter. Though he had made the Peace of the Pyrenees with Spain, it suited him to have Portugal independent as a thorn in her side. He therefore sent a secret envoy (Bastide) to urge Charles to marry Catherine and offered him a large sum of money which could be used to pay the troops which he would have to send to Portugal. But though matters had gone so far, and the treaty was in draft, there still remained important points of difference between Mello and the English commissioners.

Article 2 did not satisfy him, and he asked that the King should engage to mediate for a peace between Portugal and Holland, or defend the former from the attacks of the latter; he got what he wanted by a secret article. The commissioners objected to Charles binding himself to defend Portugal as if it were England, but Mello insisted on this, declaring that otherwise he would not make the treaty, since this condition was the chief reason for the marriage, and he appealed to the King, who ordered the demand to be conceded; it was done in article 15. The commissioners made a difficulty about keeping an English fleet on the Portuguese coast and here again Mello referred to Charles, saying that Portugal could not subsist without her trade with the colonies, so that if the coast were not cleared of pirates, she would continue to suffer more losses by sea than an invading army by land could cause her. The King attended to him, and by article 16 promised to send ships for the purpose, and that whenever Portugal was pressed by the enemy, all English vessels at Tangier or in the Mediteranean should go to her aid. Tangier, was the main obstacle to a complete agreement, because Clarendon, who directed the negotiations with Mello, feared that the Portuguese would lose it at any moment to the Moors, or refuse to hand it over, but in exchange for a declaration by Charles, Mello agreed that it should be surrendered before the marriage, and it was settled by article 4 that on its delivery, the fleet sent to receive it should transport the Infanta to England. By a document dated June 22nd, Charles declared

Catherine to be his wife before the signature of the treaty, to expedite the matter and avoid sending to Rome for a dispensation, which Portuguese law would require if she were betrothed in Portugal. It was however, provided that if the clauses in the treaty which had to be performed previous to her embarkation were not carried out, the declaration was to be void. One of these stipulated that half the dowry should be put on board before the Infanta embarked, but this was not enforced ; a year was allowed for the payment of the remainder, but, owing to the poverty of the treasury, the last instalment was not paid until many years later ; the dowries of Queens were, however, by no means always paid in full. The treaty was signed on June 23rd, 1661. It confirmed those of 1642 and 1654, and added to the extensive privileges granted to the English by those conventions, but contained a guarantee of support, not found in the earlier ones, which was now indispensable, because, after the Peace of the Pyrenees, Spain found herself free to concentrate all her forces against Portugal. The engagement of Charles to defend the latter with all his strength, as if she were England, had no time limit, it has been successfully invoked by the Portuguese on several occasions and is regarded as still binding, while the promise to mediate a peace between Portugal and Holland was performed in the treaty of 6th August, 1661. Moreover in addition to an English guarantee of her independence, Portuguese secured the secret assistance of Louis and the open help of England, in the shape of men and money for the war with Spain, the successful issue of which justified the sacrifices which were made to secure them.

Nevertheless, the treaty, necessary as it was, proved very unpopular. The Portuguese blamed their government severely for the cession of Tangier and

Bombay and their historians have ventilated other grievances arising out of it.

Hence, when the draft of the Treaty was submitted to the Council of State, the Queen Regent ordered the Secretary to refrain from reading the articles concerning Tangier.[1]

The possession of Tangier was only important to a power having interests in the Mediterranean and Portugal had none in that sea, but the Portuguese had won the place in 1471, it was a home to thousands of them, and they were shocked to see the churches at the mercy of heretics who hated Catholicism.

The village and island of Bombay brought no profit to the state, but its cession cut in two the Portuguese settlements on the west coast and established a trading rival in the midst of them. No one foresaw that it would prove to be a first step in the foundation of a British dominion in India.

By article 14 of the treaty, Charles agreed that if ever Ceylon fell into English hands, he would hand over the city of Colombo to Portugal, its former owner, but when the island was eventually ceded by Holland to Great Britain in 1802 at the Peace of Amiens, this stipulation was, perhaps not unnaturally, ignored. Again, by the secret article, Charles promised to compel the Dutch to restore any fortresses taken by them from the Portuguese after his mediation had been accepted, but he failed to secure the restitution to them of Cochin and Cananor, though in this case the delay in the surrender of Bombay gave him some excuse. Another, and a legitimate grievance derived from the English abandonment of Tangier to the Moors in 1684, after an occupation of twenty-two years. The Portuguese asked that it should be returned to them, and their patriotic and religious sentiments were outraged by the

[1] *Archivo Historico Portugues*, vol. 6, p. 225.

refusal; they could not accept as a satisfactory excuse the English fear that they might be unable to hold the town against the Moors, or might transfer it to France.

Bibliography.

Borges de Castro, J. *Collecção dos Tratados . . . . . entre a corôa de Portugal e as mais potencias desde* 1640, etc. Vol. I and IX, Lisbon, 1856 and 1872.

Santarem, Visconde de, and Rebello da Silva, J. A. *Quadro Elementar das relações politicas e diplomaticas de Portugal com as diversas potencias do mundo.* Vol. 17, Lisbon, 1869.

Roma du Bocage, C. *Subsidios para o estudo das relações exteriores de Portugal em seguida á Restauração* (1640-1649). Lisbon 1916.

Prestage, E. *The diplomatic relations of Portugal with France, England and Holland from* 1640 *to* 1668, Watford, 1925.

————*A embaixada de Tristão de Mendonça Furtado a Holanda em* 1641. Coimbra, 1920. (*Instituto*, Vol. 67.)

————*O Conde de Castelmelhor e a retrocessão de Tanger a Portugal.* Coimbra, 1917. (*Boletim da 2a classe da Academia das Sciencias de Lisboa*, Vol. 11.)

————*O. Dr. Antonio de Sousa de Macedo, Residente de Portugal em Londres* (1642-1646) Lisbon, 1916. (*Boletim da 2a classe da Academia das Sciencias de Lisboa*, Vol. 10.)

Guernsey Jones. *Beginnings of the oldest European alliance— England and Portugal* 1640-1661 (*American Hist. Association Reports* 1916, I. 410).

Shafaat Ahmad Khan. *The Anglo-Portuguese negotiations relating to Bombay*, 1660-1677. (*Journal of Indian History*, September, 1922.)

Albrecht, J. *Die hierat Karl II von England mit Katharina von Bragança*, (*Bremer Wissenschaftlichen Gesellschaft*, March 1928).

Grose, Clyde L. *The Anglo-Portuguese marriage of 1662.* (*Hispanic American Review*, August, 1930).

Rebello da Silva L. A. *Historia de Portugal nos seculos XVII e XVIII*, Vols. 4 and 5. Lisbon, 1869, 1871.

Netscher, P. M. *Les Hollandais au Brésil.* Hague 1853.

CHAPTER V.

The Treaties of 1703.

Of the six lecturers who have taken part in this course, I have the easiest task—a survey of the three treaties made in 1703, which in English history are frequently called the Methuen Treaties. To understand their significance, it is necessary to glance at the great European problem of the time. This was the settlement of the succession to the vast Spanish dominions which was vacant by the death of the last male of the Spanish Hapsburg line in 1700. There were originally three claimants by female descent, but by 1700 there were only two. One was the Austrian Hapsburg, the Emperor Leopold, or rather his second son, the Archduke Charles, who had been substituted for his father in the hope of disarming the jealousy which would be excited in Europe by the union in one hand of the Austrian and the Spanish inheritance. Europe had no desire to see a renewal of the vast empire of Charles V. The accession of the Archduke Charles would merely continue a state of things with which Europe had been familiar for a century and a half : one Hapsburg line in Austria, and another separate line in Spain. The other claimant in the strict sense was the French Dauphin, the son of Louis XIV by his first marriage with the Infanta Maria Theresa. It was obvious that Europe would never tolerate the accession of the Dauphin, the heir to the most powerful monarchy of the age, to the throne of Spain with its appendages, the Netherlands, the Italian provinces and a vast colonial empire. All that could be hoped from insistence upon the Dauphin's claim was to snatch for France some fragments of the Spanish inheritance, preferably those in Italy. This was the original policy of Louis XIV, who sought in the two successive partition treaties of 1698 and 1700 to gain what he could for France. But there were two resolute opponents of partition. One was the Emperor Leopold, who refused to accept even the second partition treaty of 1700, though it offered to the Archduke the whole inheritance outside Italy. The Emperor clung to the old family tradition, maintained for generations and fortified by constant intermarriages, that on the extinction of either of the main Hapsburg lines the other should succeed. And the policy of partition, which William III had advocated as the only way of evading a great European war, found another vehement opponent in the proud nobles and people of Spain, who regarded the maintenance of the undivided empire to be not only their glory but their duty. It was this passion for unity and for the continued predominance of Castile which extorted from the dying Charles II of Spain the final testament by which, on condition that there should be no union with the crown of France, his whole undivided inheritance was bequeathed, not to the Dauphin, but to the Dauphin's second son, Philip of Anjou. The motive for this startling and un- expected expedient was to tempt Louis XIV to drop his schemes for the aggrandisement of France by offering a far greater aggrandisement to the house of Bourbon. It was shrewdly reckoned that France was the only power strong enough to foil those projects of partition which France herself had hitherto promoted.

It is unnecessary to tell the often told tale of what followed. Louis XIV, on the plea that circumstances had completely changed, repudiated the partition treaty which he had concluded a few months before, and accepted the bequest of the undivided Spanish inheritance for his grandson. And for a moment it appeared that this bold decision would not encounter formidable opposition. The Tory party in England and the Republican party in Holland were strong enough to hold William III in check, and both parties were inclined to regard the present settlement in Spain as rather better than the recent partition which the King-Stadtholder had negotiated. It was inevitable that the Emperor should go to war on behalf of the rejected Hapsburg claim, but Austria single-handed was impotent to do more than attack the Milanese, and even that enterprise was not likely to be successful. It was only gradually that the arrogant and reckless conduct of Louis XIV, which threatened both English and Dutch mercantile interests and the Protestant succession in England, convinced the two Maritime Powers that twin Bourbon rulers in France and in the undivided Spanish Empire would create intolerable conditions. The consequent reaction in public opinion enabled William III to conclude the Grand Alliance with the Emperor in September, 1691. Its basic condition was that the Bourbon King of Spain must be deprived of the Netherlands and of those possessions in Italy which, added to the southern ports of France and the eastern and southern ports of Spain, would make the Bourbon powers supreme in the Mediterranean. Circumstances had perforce convinced the Emperor Leopold that partition, which he had hitherto rejected, was better than total exclusion.

How did all this affect the relations between England and Portugal ? The connection is both intimate and vital. For such an extensive war as was now planned, naval action in the Mediterranean was imperative and might well be decisive. But experience in the seventeenth century wars had proved that, without a careening port in the vicinity, English or Dutch intervention in the Mediterranean could only be fitful and intermittent. Now that we had given up Tangier, that attractive part of the dowry of Catharine of Braganza, we had no such harbour under our own control. The only harbour not in the hands of our enemies which could serve our purpose was Lisbon, and hence it was necessary for us to secure free admission of our ships of war to the Tagus. Such admission would be impossible if Portugal should be allied with the Bourbon powers or should decide to remain neutral. Not for the first time, geography enabled Portugal to play a dominant part in European history.

Normally, there should have been no difficulty in securing the Portuguese alliance. The successive treaties of 1642, 1654 and 1661, which were the subject of the last lecture, had bound Portugal very closely to England, both economically and politically. It is true that a powerful impulse towards the recovery of Portuguese independence had come from France, but France had deserted Portugal by the Treaty of the Pyrenees, and the final recognition of independence in 1668 had been extorted from Spain very largely by the military and diplomatic intervention of England. Not only gratitude but continued friction with Spain about frontiers both in the Peninsula and in South America, together with the fear that Spain might seek to reduce her neighbour once more into subjection, impelled Portugal to cling to the English alliance in spite of the dividing force of religion. Hostile critics in later times declared that Portugal had sunk to the position of a client state. More than once had England, in the seventeenth century, used the Tagus as if the river had belonged to this country. A people possessing the proud traditions of Portugal in the fifteenth and sixteenth centuries could not but feel their dependence rather galling. No state, however intimate and cordial its alliance with another, likes to draw necessaries of life from an alien or to have its policy dictated from outside. The first move was in the direction of economic independence. Portugal produced plenty of wool of its own and could import more from Castile, but its artisans lacked the necessary skill for working up the raw materials. The conditions resembled those of England in the fourteenth century, and the expedients adopted were similar in character. Just as Edward III had imported Flemish cloth-workers into England,[1] so the Portuguese government invited the immigration of skilled workmen from England. As soon as the foundations had been laid of native manufacture, two successive edicts were issued in 1684 and 1685 to protect it by prohibiting the importation of certain kinds of woollen goods, and by ordering people to wear cloths made at home.[2] As the principal exports from England to Portugal consisted of woollen goods, these edicts were resented in England. But they did not constitute a breach of the letter of any treaties and, as long as Portugal was politically

[1]On the economic policy of Edward III, see E. Lipson, *History of the English Woollen and Worsted Industry*, pp. 12-15.

[2]John Methuen thus described these protective measures: "The Portuguese, finding their money exported to England in return for our goods, despairing of ballancing our trade by their wines, etc., and considering the quantity of very good wooll which Portugall produces and the convenience of having what wooll they pleased from Spain, they resolved to prohibit the woollen manufactures of England and sett up the same in their kingdom, where their wooll was very cheap. They began with prohibiting all cloth hats, stockens and some other sorts, but forbore the prohibition of Bays and the rest till they could attain the making of them." (B. M., Add. MSS., 29,590, f. 394.)

docile, such resentment did not weaken the alliance. The possibility of political defection did not arise until the war of the Spanish Succession approached.

If the union of France and Spain under kings of a common dynasty involved dangers to England and Holland, it was still more formidable to Portugal. If the two great states acted cordially together, as seemed probable and indeed at the outset inevitable, Portuguese independence, never very secure against Spain alone, would be at their mercy. Nor could Portugal, without very powerful allies, venture to oppose their union, and for a time, owing to the original attitude of the Maritime Powers, there seemed no prospect of gaining such allies. It was not surprising in these circumstances that Portugal sought to secure a precarious safety by submission. France had very good reason to desire a breach of the alliance between England and Portugal, which, in a short-sighted moment after the Restoration of 1660, she had contributed to bring about. If Portugal could be induced or coerced to close her ports to the English navy, a very serious danger to France would be averted. It was, therefore, a triumph of French diplomacy when, in June, 1701, the terrified Pedro II, in order to conciliate a king whom he dared not defy, concluded a treaty with France by which he undertook to acknowledge and support Philip V as King of the whole Spanish dominions and to close his ports against the ships of all hostile powers.[1] The only condition which the Portuguese king was able to extort in return, was that France should supply sufficient naval and

[1]Pedro's alarm was well founded. At the moment when Louis XIV was endeavouring to conciliate Portugal, Philip V and his advisers were of opinion that the opportunity had come to re-conquer that kingdom. Louis had to exert all his authority at Madrid to extort Spanish consent to the making of a treaty by which, *inter alia*, France guaranteed the integrity and independence of Portugal. See Baudrillart, *Philippe V et la Cour de France*, I, p. 90.

military force to defend Portugal against any state which might take umbrage at this treaty.

When England, a few months later, was driven under provocation from France into the Grand Alliance, this Franco-Portuguese treaty threatened to be a very serious stumbling-block. Co-operation with Austria in Italy was impossible without a naval force in the Mediterranean, and the closing of the Portuguese ports would render the sending of such a force very difficult and might make its operations ineffective. Therefore, the English ministers decided that, either by cajolery or by coercion, the opening of these ports must be secured. At the moment, England was represented at Lisbon by Paul Methuen, who had succeeded his father, John Methuen, as Envoy Extraordinary in 1697. In view of the importance of the issue, the father, who had been Envoy during the previous European war (1692-1697) and since his recall had been Chancellor of Ireland, was sent out in 1702 to reinforce the son. In order to give his mission increased weight and dignity, he was authorised to assume the higher rank of Ambassador, if and when he thought fit. His primary instruction was to demand imperatively that Lisbon and all other Portuguese harbours should be open to the English fleet. He was also to lay stress upon the French king's recognition of the Pretender, and to say that, if Portugal adhered to the French treaty, there could be no continuance of friendship with England. Finally, he was to urge the king to join the Grand Alliance, and if he should desire any advantage, such as the extension of his kingdom, Methuen was authorised to assure him: (1) that England and the States General would use all their influence with the Emperor to obtain the acceptance of any reasonable demands, and (2) that the Maritime Powers would be willing to give him the same security for his dominions as had been promised by France. If the reply to these overtures should be unsatisfactory, he was to declare that a mere fulfilment of existing treaties with England and Holland would not be regarded as adequate.[1]

The story of the subsequent negotiations is not very complicated, and may be read in the despatches of the two Methuens to the Secretary of State.[2] They had to co-operate with the Austrian and Dutch ministers at Lisbon, but the long and intimate connection of England with Portugal threw the main burden upon the English envoys.[3] John Methuen abstained at the outset from assuming ambassadorial rank in order to have greater freedom of movement. He relied upon the threat of abrupt departure to hasten the decisions of the Portuguese court. He soon found that more depended upon the actual balance of forces than upon diplomatic arguments. Portugal would not undertake to admit the English fleet until it was known whether France was prepared to send the stipulated naval aid. Accordingly, John Methuen quitted Lisbon on 10th June, (N.S.) (he had arrived on 7th May), and hurried home to expedite the departure of the fleet which was being prepared to co-operate with a Dutch squadron in an attack upon Cadiz. The arrival of the allied fleet off the coast in August, though it unfortunately passed the mouth of the Tagus in the dark (a blunder from the diplomatic point of view), combined with the failure of France to send any counterbalancing force, enabled John

---

[1]These instructions, dated 6th April (O.S.), 1702, are in B. M., Add. MSS., 29,590, f. 434.

[2]The majority of these despatches are to be found, not in the Record Office, but in the British Museum, (Add. MSS., 29,590).

[3]John Methuen reported in August, 1702, that the Austrian and Dutch ministers were inclined to resent his prominence in the negotiation.

Methuen, who had now returned to Lisbon, to report on 25th August (O.S.), that the King of Portugal had denounced his treaty with France and that he was as free from obligation to Louis XIV as if the treaty had never been made. It was now possible to raise the vital question of the adhesion of Portugal to the Grand Alliance. If Sir George Rooke had been successful in his attack upon Cadiz, there would have been no doubt as to the Portuguese decision, and it was a great blow to the Methuens that the enterprise ended in discreditable failure. Fortunately for the allies, the failure was redeemed by a brilliant success at Vigo, where a number of French ships were destroyed and a considerable amount of Spanish treasure from the Indies was captured. This was sufficient to put an end to Portuguese hesitation, but there still remained the difficult task of fixing the terms of the extended alliance. More than six months of strenuous diplomacy were required before a treaty could be adjusted to the satisfaction of the various powers concerned.

The primary and very natural demand of Portugal was for security. Pedro II could not afford to be left at the end of the war to face a hostile and exasperated King of Spain. Therefore the allies must undertake to drive Philip V out of the Peninsula, and must pledge themselves to conclude no peace which did not insist upon the exclusion of the Bourbons from the Spanish throne. As a pledge for the performance of these promises, the Archduke must be proclaimed as Charles III of Spain and must come in person to claim his crown and to join the composite army, which was to conquer his kingdom for him. The same desire for security prompted the second demand, that the Maritime Powers should give Portugal a definite guarantee of territorial integrity and the assurance of assistance against external attack. Austria was too far away to be useful in this respect, and moreover, Austria was not a naval power. Finally, the Portuguese king and his ministers demanded substantial gains for their own state. The northern and eastern frontiers of Portugal must be expanded at the expense of Spain, and in South America the Hapsburg king must recognise the Rio de la Plata as the southern boundary of Brazil and must abandon all Spanish claims to territory on the north side of that river.

Of these demands, the first, the expulsion of the Bourbon King, was by far the most important and had the most far-reaching results, but it was admitted to be a *sine qua non*, and could only be refused by dropping the whole project. The second demand, for a defensive treaty, was merely a corollary of the first, and gave rise to no difficulties. There were inevitable disputes as to the contributions of the several allies to the joint army which was to be prepared for the invasion of Spain. But by far the most prolonged and acrimonious controversy was provoked by the territorial demands of Portugal. If Charles III was to make good his claim to the Spanish crown, he must not only conquer the country but must gain the allegiance of his future subjects. From this latter point of view, it would be in the highest degree inauspicious to begin his reign by sacrificing Spanish territory and interests to a neighbouring state which was regarded in Spain with mingled dislike and contempt. Hence the chief opposition to the proposed treaty came from Austria, in whose interest it had been planned. The Emperor Leopold, whose most immediate design was to acquire the Italian provinces for his son, was not eager to send the Archduke on a distant and dangerous campaign in the Spanish Peninsula. But his cardinal objection was to the cession of Spanish territory and claims. He refused to admit that the Portuguese alliance was of such imperative importance as to require such extensive and humiliating sacrifices. He was willing to give cessions in South America, but none in the Peninsula. The English and Dutch envoys, who acted in this dispute as mediators, had great difficulties, on the one hand in moderating the excessive demands of Portugal, and on the other in convincing Austria that substantial concessions were necessary in the interests of the Grand Alliance.[1] John Methuen was so exasperated by the protracted delay in the negotiations, that he made the second of his demonstrative departures from Lisbon on 11th April, 1703. During his absence, the conflicting parties finally came to terms, and it was Paul Methuen who signed on behalf of England the two treaties which were concluded on 16th May.

One of these treaties was the defensive alliance concluded by Portugal with England and the Dutch Republic. It had given rise to no disputes, it attracted little attention at the time, and was so completely forgotten in England that, at a later date, ministers had difficulty in finding a copy, and at one moment went so far as to deny its existence. All that need be noted about it, and it is a proof of the commanding position of Portugal in 1703, is that it contained an apparently irrelevant clause providing that all privileges enjoyed by the English and Dutch in Portugal should be enjoyed by Portuguese residents

[1] It is interesting to note that the ministers of the Maritime Powers, while discussing the gains to be given to Portugal, kept an eye on the interests of their own states. They were especially eager that Portugal should obtain the attractive harbour of Vigo. This, as John Methuen pointed out, would be of advantage to the English and Dutch traders, because it would give them an open port in the north of Portugal, and thus enable them to escape the " bad and uncertain " bar of Oporto. (to Nottingham, 29th August (O.S.), 1702, in B. M., Add. MSS., 29,590, f. 106). In the end the treaty of 16th May, 1703, promised to Portugal the cession of Badajoz, Albuquerque, Valencia, Alcantara, Guarda, Tuy and Vigo, in addition to the Spanish territory north of the river Plate.

in England and Holland.[1] The other treaty, a quadruple treaty signed by Austria as well as by the plenipotentiaries of the Maritime Powers, bound Portugal to the Grand Alliance and pledged the allies to expel the Bourbons from Spain. It is impossible to exaggerate the contemporary importance of this treaty, which changed the whole character and aims of the European war. Without it, Austria would probably have failed to gain her Italian possessions, at any rate those in the south of Italy, and England would certainly not have acquired Gibraltar and Minorca. It was perhaps, the misfortune, rather than the fault, of the allies that, while they took the gains which the treaty gave them, they failed to pay the stipulated price for them. In the end, they found the expulsion of Philip from Spain to be beyond their powers, and when the Archduke Charles succeeded to the Austrian dominions on the death of his brother, it ceased from some points of view to be even desirable. In the later stages of the war, this Methuen treaty of 16th May, 1703, gave rise to an embittered party controversy in England. Although the treaty had been concluded under the direction of a High Tory Secretary of State, the Earl of Nottingham,[2] it was the Whigs who clung to its essential formula, " no peace with a Bourbon king in Spain," and it was the Tory party which condemned the treaty as an impolitic departure from the original aims of the Grand Alliance. The treaty, according to Professor Trevelyan's estimate, added four needless years to the war, and Portugal

[1]Pombal laid great stress upon this clause in his rather acrimonious controversies with the British government.

[2]On Nottingham's consistency in this matter, see Trevelyan, *Blenheim*, p. 303, and *The Peace and the Protestant Succession*, p. 195. He was the only Tory who opposed the peace policy of the Tory ministry on the ground that it was contrary to English interests to leave a Bourbon on the Spanish throne.

emerged from the peace-making at Utrecht both unrewarded and endangered. None of the territorial promises in Europe could possibly be fulfilled, and the little state was left with nothing but paper guarantees to protect it against a justly indignant Bourbon king in Spain. Arguments can be used, and have been used, to defend the part played by England in the Utrecht settlement. Professor Trevelyan, in his last volume, has said all that can fairly be said on behalf of Bolingbroke and his associates, but even as told by him the story has an evil savour.

After the conclusion of the two treaties of 16th May, John Methuen returned to Lisbon in September, 1703, carrying with him the English ratifications. He now assumed, at last, the character of Ambassador, which he had hitherto abstained from taking. His avowed business was to superintend the organisation of the allied army which was to undertake the invasion of Spain. His only commercial instruction was to extort from the prospective Charles III a favourable treaty with Spain, and especially the grant to England of the *asiento* for the carrying on of the slave trade with the West Indies. But he found in Portugal an apparently unexpected desire for a mercantile bargain. Ever since the accession of William III had led to wars with France, the importation of French wines into England had been either prohibited or subjected to heavy duties. The result had been an increased demand for Portuguese wines, both port and Madeira. This had enabled Portugal to pay for English imports in goods, instead of in bullion, and had thus partially redressed what was regarded, in the peninsular kingdom, as the adverse balance of trade. Now that the connection with England had been drawn closer by Portuguese adhesion to the Grand Alliance, there was a desire to obtain permanence for this temporary gain. The obvious price to be offered was the removal of the restrictions imposed for the last eighteen years upon the import of the woollen goods which had for centuries been England's staple product. Such a bargain had several times been mooted in England and, though Methuen had neither instructions nor authority to conclude such an agreement, he had no hesitation in signing on 27th December, 1703, the treaty which has given to his name a permanent prominence in English history.

It is needless to expatiate on the error into which so many English historians have fallen, of regarding what is generally known as *the* Methuen Treaty as part of the bribe given to induce Portugal to join the Grand Alliance. The simple facts of chronology, not fully made clear even by Professor Trevelyan, are fatal to this contention. Portugal joined the Grand Alliance on 16th May; the commercial treaty was not signed until 27th December. The later treaty was the result of, and not the motive for, its predecessor. Methuen's despatches make it clear that the initiative in concluding the mercantile agreement was taken by Portugal. But he was right in assuming that it would be cordially welcomed in England. It was ratified without hesitation, and John Methuen's conduct in concluding it without authority and without reference to the home government was applauded by his employers.

This treaty of December, 1703, is the shortest, simplest and perhaps the most famous of all commercial treaties. Adam Smith quoted it in full and devoted the great part of a chapter to it. It influenced British policy for a century, and on two important occasions it occupied a prominent place in party and parliamentary controversies. Its terms are easy to state. English woollens were to be admitted to Portugal as they had been in the past, and the duty on Portuguese wines was always to be a third less than that imposed upon French wines. As a matter of fact, the difference of duties had been in the past ten years, was at the time of the conclusion of the treaty, and was frequently in the future, greater than the third stipulated in the treaty.

You are all doubtless aware of the legend which attributes to this Methuen treaty the taste for port wine, and the consequent prevalence of gout in England. You may also know that one of the causes of Scottish discontent with the Act of Union was that it forced Scotsmen to pay the higher duties upon the French wines which they were accustomed to drink. I hope that you are also familiar with the famous lines in which a patriotic Scot gave expression to this discontent.

" Firm and erect the Caledonian stood,
    Good was his claret, and his mutton good.
    ' Let him drink port,' the *British* statesman cried :
    He drank the poison, and his spirit died."

The legend that the Methuen treaty generated a taste for port is not strictly accurate, as the preferential duties on Portuguese wines date back to 1690, and the treaty of 1703 only confirmed them ; but it is sufficiently accurate to justify the legend. But it is quite true that Scotland resented the treaty. For many generations, every Scotsman who could afford the luxury of patriotism deemed it his duty to stock his cellar with excellent claret, and the best wines from Bordeaux found their market, not in London, but in Leith. It is true that this tradition has in recent years given way to the habit of drinking whisky and soda at meals and port after dinner. But perhaps the newly formed Home Rule Party in Scotland will turn their attention to the revival of the taste for claret and of the wine trade between Bordeaux and Leith.

In spite of its apparent simplicity, the interpretation of the Methuen Treaty gave rise to controversies. The famous Marquis of Pombal went so far as to denounce subsequent increases in the duty on port wine as a breach of the treaty. In this he was obviously as wrong as he was in his contention that the treaty had been made to induce Portugal to join the allies. In the letter which John Methuen wrote to excuse his unauthorised signature of the treaty, he expressly pointed out that there was no limit to the duties that might be imposed upon Portuguese wine, provided that wine from France had to pay the additional third.[1] As a matter of fact, the clause about wine was perfectly clear. It is true that it contains the unusual phrase that Portuguese wines are to be admitted on the prescribed terms " for ever hereafter " (*à l'avenir pour toujours*). But no treaty, least of all a commercial treaty, could possibly be eternal, and no treaty could deprive the British House of Commons of its control of taxation. And the peccant words were deprived of all binding force by the subsequent sentence, which declared that, if England at any time should fail to impose the extra duty upon France, Portugal would be free to renew its prohibition of the import of English woollens. But the clause about wool was not equally free from doubt. It stipulated that English woollen manufacturers should be admitted " as was accustomed till they were prohibited " (*comme il à été usité jusqu' au moment*, etc.). Were these words merely descriptive of past freedom of admission, or did they involve an obligation on Portugal not to increase the duties levied upon these goods before the first restrictive edict in 1684 ? England asserted, as did Adam Smith, that Portugal was bound not to raise

[1]This letter is printed in *Transactions of the Royal Historical Society*, Fourth Series, Vol. XVI.

the duties which had been paid before the prohibition. On the whole, with some grumbling, the Portuguese accepted this interpretation of the clause. But there were other dubious points. England contended, again with some success, that admission into Portugal carried with it admission to the Portuguese colonies, and based upon this a claim, which Portugal tried vainly to dispute, to a right of direct trade with Brazil. But the most monstrous interpretation of the clause on the part of English merchants was that, as no mention was made of other traders, it gave to England an exclusive right to import woollen cloth into Portugal. This contention was resolutely rejected by Portugal, and in the course of the eighteenth century both Dutch and French manufactures became serious rivals of English goods in the Lisbon market.

The Methuen Treaty, identified with national hostility to France, became, as Charles Fox called it, " the idol of the Whig party." It was the main basis of their opposition to Bolingbroke's attempt to conclude a commercial treaty with France in 1713 and to the treaty which Pitt actually concluded in 1786. Even though Pitt's treaty provided that French wines should be admitted on payment of the same duties as those at present paid by Portuguese wines, the Parliament so far clung to the Methuen Treaty that, in the Act of 1787, the duty on Portuguese wines was lowered by the stipulated third. The subsequent wars with France and the close association with Portugal in the Peninsular War kept the treaty alive until 1840. This long duration for nearly a century and a half, combined with its prominence in party debates, has undoubtedly given to the third Methuen treaty a reputation which it hardly deserves. Adam Smith discussed it at length as if it was a model commercial treaty. As a matter of fact, it was not a comprehensive treaty like that of 1654, but rather two supplementary clauses added on to that great treaty. I have read volumes of eighteenth century State Papers in which British merchants formulated their complaints against the measures taken by Pombal to free his country from its excessive dependence upon foreign manufactures and foreign imports. Nearly all these complaints are directed against alleged breaches of the treaty of 1654, and there are hardly any references to the treaty of 1703. The really important treaty of 1703 was that of 16th May, which brought the Spanish Succession War to the Peninsula and profoundly affected the history of Europe. It is one of the anomalies of history that this treaty should have so long been mixed up with, and in a way overshadowed by, the lesser treaty with which it had only an indirect association, and that the name of " Methuen " should be almost monopolised by what John Methuen himself must have regarded as a rather minor achievement.

Author's Note.

The most complete study of the Methuen treaty of 27th December, 1703, has been made in two articles which Dr. Hans Schorer contributed to the *Zeitschrift für die gesamte Staatswissens- chaft* in 1903 (Vol. LIX). The main conclusion of both articles is that the importance of the treaty, both from the political and from the economic point of view, has been grossly exaggerated by tradition, by politicians, and by historians. But there is a curious inequality between the two articles. In the first he demonstrates that simple chronology is sufficient to demolish the current view that the concession as to Portuguese wine on 27th December was the bribe given to induce Portugal to adhere to the Grand Alliance on 16th May. At the same time he contends that the dependence of Portugal upon England—which some writers describe as economic and political servitude—dates, not from 1703, but from the marriage treaty of Catharine of Braganza in 1661. Of the Commonwealth treaty of 1654 he makes in this article no mention at all. He also holds that John Methuen was commissioned in August, 1703, to conclude the commercial treaty (*zu diesem Zweck*) and he shows no knowledge of his presence or activity at Lisbon in 1702 and in the earlier months of 1703. By the time that he wrote the second article (much the better of the two), Dr. Schorer had widened and clarified his knowledge. He had discovered the treaties of 1642 and 1654, had clearly grasped the differences which made the latter treaty far the more important of the two, and was now prepared to assert that the latter treaty (not the marriage treaty of 1661) was the Magna Carta on which English traders in Lisbon depended for their mercantile and their personal privileges. He points out very aptly that in the controversies with Pombal the English complaints are all directed against alleged breaches of the treaty of 1654 and that the Methuen treaty is hardly mentioned. He has also learned in the interval that John Methuen's commission to Portugal (on his return to diplomatic activity) was issued in 1702 and not in August, 1703, and that he took an active part in promoting the treaty of 16th May, though it was signed by his son during his own temporary absence from Lisbon. On the whole, allowing for the rather odd discrepancies between the two articles, and for the fact that Dr. Schorer depended almost wholly upon printed authorities, his articles must be regarded as a notable, though little known, contribution to our knowledge of Anglo-Portuguese relations.

CHAPTER VI.

Portuguese Expansion Overseas, its causes and results.

Portugal owes her place in world history to four achievements, the first two of which are more spectacular and more widely recognised than the others. These are the ocean voyages, in which she discovered the coasts of almost half the globe in less than one hundred years, and those martial successes in the East which gave her a monopoly of the spice trade with Europe for the same period. Her other two titles to fame are the missionary enterprise, fostered by her Kings, which she displayed, and her colonisation of Brazil, a country as large as the United States and embracing much more than a half of South America.

It is the object of this lecture to endeavour to set out the causes and results, both to herself and to other peoples, of the expansion in three continents of a small nation whose population at its zenith in the sixteenth century did not exceed, if it reached, one million and a half.

A study of the map of Europe suggests that the geographical position of Portugal called her to the sea as a fruitful field of action, while natural features served as a wall to separate her from her neighbour. She is a narrow strip of territory on the west coast of the Iberian peninsula, her harbours are nearer to Africa and South America than any others, and the prevailing winds favour voyages under sail in those directions. In the Middle Ages, the far larger and more powerful state of Castile cut her off from the rest of the continent and removed the temptation to a waste of energy in European conflicts, because the frontier between the two, with its obstacles of mountain, river and wilderness, rendered the passage and subsistence of an invading army difficult, except at two or three points and these capable of defence.

The shores of Portugal are beaten by the full force of the Atlantic and, save for the volcanic group of the Azores, there is no land between them and America, but the adjoining ocean contains abundance of fish, so that in early times this natural food supply caused the coasts to be preferred for settlement to the interior, most of which was covered with forests and scrub. Small towns arose whose inhabitants took to the sea in increasing numbers, and these became a race of hardy mariners. In the twelfth and thirteenth centuries the visits of crusading fleets probably stirred their imagination and led them to dream of distant voyages, and their descendants found their way to Labrador and Brazil in the West and to the Moluccas and Japan in the East. Even now, the only two cities, Lisbon and Oporto, are near the sea, while the largest inland town counts but 30,000 inhabitants. If other countries with similar geographical advantages have not produced seafarers on the same scale, we must look for special reasons which account for the success of the Portuguese. We may find them in the adventurous spirit of the race which was undaunted by the storms of the ocean, the sea of darkness of the Arabs, and also in its moderation in food and drink,[1] which produced a virile stock. To these favourable conditions may be added a relative freedom from internal strife and the leadership of a man of genius, Henry the Navigator, who pursued his aim of maritime exploration for forty years, lived like an austere monk and never married. The main reasons which have led to the expansion of other peoples, great poverty, over-population or an unfruitful soil, did not operate in the case of Portugal.

The Portuguese were Crusaders before they became navigators, their country was born during the struggle to recover the Peninsula from the Moors, and Portugal preserved the crusading spirit down to the last quarter of the sixteenth century, that is long after other nations had abandoned it for purely material aims. In 1578, King Sebastian lost his life and army at the battle of Alcacer Kebir in the attempt to win Morocco for the law of Christ and prevent the Turks from establishing themselves on the Atlantic.[2]

When her history begins, Portugal was a county between the rivers Minho and Douro, part of the kingdom of Leon, and ruled by Henry, a Burgundian knight, who had come to the Peninsula to fight for the Cross and seek his fortune. Henry's son, Alfonso Henriques, won independence for his county, made it a nation and himself a king. In 1139, he strengthened his position by a victory at Ourique over a large Moorish host and, according to an old legend, took as arms five shields in the form of a Cross at the bidding of Our Lord, who had appeared to him on the eve of

[1]The historian, Duarte Nunes de Lião quotes Strabo as saying that the Lusitanians drank water and not wine. He adds that the Portuguese in the sixteenth century were more abstemious than other peoples, after the manner of their ancient Kings, whose cupbearers took more pains to seek good waters for their masters than good wines. *Descripção de Portugal*, Lisbon, 1610, fol. 33 vo.

[2]*Boletim da 2a classe da Academia das Sciencias de Lisboa*, vol. 1, p. 293.

the battle and promised him success. Eight years later he captured Lisbon by the aid of a crusading fleet from the north of Europe which was on its way to Palestine. His successors gradually extended their frontiers southward and about 1250 Muslim dominion came to an end and Portugal attained her present limits, which have remained practically unchanged ever since, a fact almost, if not quite, unique in history.

The growth and consolidation of the little realm was interrupted a century later by efforts of her neighbour to reincorporate her, but the victory of Aljubarrota (14th August, 1385) secured her against molestation for another two hundred years and in 1415, she was able to enter on her career of expansion overseas. ʃIn view of her record, it is not strange that the principal reason for the attack on Ceuta should have been a crusading one and the penetration of Morocco was carried on at intervals during the next hundred years with the same idea. The chief towns on the coast and part of the interior were gradually occupied or became tributary, though a nationalist revival compelled the Portuguese to relax their hold in the third decade of the sixteenth century.

In 1418, Prince Henry inaugurated the ocean voyages and at his death in 1460, his mariners had sailed down and mapped the west coast of Africa as far as Sierra Leone, while Madeira, the Azores and some of the Cape Verde islands had been colonised and churches built in them. To the world, the value of his achievement was that it destroyed the terrors inspired by the ocean and proved that, contrary to the current opinion, the torrid zone was habitable by man. In addition to his scientfiic and commercial aims, Henry was inspired by the desire to spread the Christian faith and combat Islam by attacking it on the flank and in the rear, and successive Popes granted spiritual favours to those who took part in the crusade and bestowed on the Kings of Portugal exclusive rights over the Infidel lands they discovered as far as the Indies, on condition that they spread the knowledge of the Gospel in those parts.

Henry's policy of expansion was not popular at first ; men in high places took the common-sense view that a poor country could not afford to employ its energies in distant adventure and, though the Prince defrayed the expense of the early voyages out of his own purse and from the revenues of the Order of Christ of which he was governor, the common folk murmured against him as though he were taking their money, but the gradual increase of trade and the slaves his sailors brought home, converted his opponents so far that they hailed him as a second Alexander and began to fit out ships on their own account.

From the middle of the fifteenth century, the profits from West Africa and the Atlantic islands grew steadily; sugar from Madeira began to be exported to foreign countries and the policy of expansion became a national one. Unlike his followers, Henry did not seek cheap labour for the fields of Portugal, he wanted natives to act as guides and interpreters to his explorers, but he was as keenly interested in commercial development as any merchant. According to Cadamosto, he took a quarter of the profits of a voyage made by those who equipped their own vessels, for by royal privilege no one could go to West Africa without his leave and he acquired other monopolies, and yet died deeply in debt because he was a generous giver and for the first twenty years his explorations gave no return.

Before his death, crusading was abandoned, because experience showed that it hindered evangelisation and trade, slaves were no longer taken by force, but bought from the Arabs and others who had carried on the business for centuries and friendly relations were established with the native tribes.

The work of exploration went on and it was pursued by men trained in Henry's school. In the reign of Afonso V it was done indirectly by means of a lease of the Guinea trade by which the lessee agreed to discover 100 leagues of coast annually, and under this contract the new found parts were extended to Cape St. Catharine, two degrees south of the Equator. Under John II and his successors the voyages of discovery came to be a royal undertaking and they were made by captains appointed by the monarchs who took with them minute instructions called *Regiments*. By the erection of the fort of Mina, our Elmina, John secured control of a goodly part of the trade in gold dust which used to go overland to the Mediterranean and the wealth he obtained from this source enabled him to build up a complete maritime organisation. But even before this and immediately after his accession he took up the work of exploration with all Henry's zeal and had far greater success. In 1482, Diogo Cão reached the Congo and in a short time the country was opened to Christianity; the King accepted baptism and some of his successors proved zealous in their faith. They were supplied with missionaries and materials for building and furnishing churches and even with coats of arms for themselves and their chiefs, thus satisfying their desire to imitate their ally, the King of Portugal. On his second voyage, Cão got to Cape Cross in South West Africa, and in 1488, Bartholomew Dias rounded the southern extremity of the continent. At the same time, Pero da Covilhã sailed down the east coast, perhaps to Sofala, from the north and sent word that the sea route to India was practicable and his report and the result of the expedition of Dias determined that of Vasco da Gama. In 1499, the latter reached Calicut and in 1500 Cabral officially discovered Brazil on his outward voyage to India. Considerable fleets were then sent yearly to the East and they brought back cargoes of spices and other goods, which were sold at an enormous profit and the overland trade in them, which formerly went via the Red Sea and Egypt, or across Syria, was gradually diverted to the ocean route. This measure struck a staggering blow at the interests of three parties, the Muslim merchants of Calicut who shipped the spices to the Red Sea, the Sultan of Egypt who received dues on the goods as they crossed his lands and the Venetians who distributed them throughout Europe. The last named could only react by intrigue but the other two defended themselves by force. Vasco da Gama had met with hostility from Muslims in East Africa on his outward voyage and this was continued in India, the first manifestation of it being an attack on the factory which Cabral had set up at Calicut and the massacre of the inmates. The Sultan threatened to destroy the Holy Places in Palestine unless the Indian voyages were abandoned, but King Manoel was convinced that he would not carry out his threat and thus lose the profits he derived from the pilgrims to Jerusalem. So far from changing his policy the King resolved to maintain a permanent military force in the East and in 1505 sent out D. Francisco de Almeida with the title of Viceroy. In reply, the Sultan despatched a fleet to Indian waters to help his co-religionists to expel the Portuguese. Its defeat at the battle of Diu in February, 1509, and the subsequent resistance of the fortress to two Turkish sieges secured to Portugal the control of the Indian Ocean for a hundred years.

Between 1510 and 1515, Afonso de Albuquerque created the " State of India "[1] which rested on sea

[1] To the Portuguese, India meant only the west coast of the Peninsula.

power and on a chain of fortresses stretching from the shores of East Africa to Malacca and later on it included the north coast of Arabia, most of Ceylon and the Moluccas. Goa was the capital and Ormuz and Malacca the outposts; the second commanded the Persian Gulf, the third the narrow strait by which the products of the Far East and Indonesia reached the West. In the seventeenth century, the State received a further accession in a triangle of territory on the Zambese which is the origin of the present colony of Mozambique while the so-called empire of Monomotapa in Central Africa was made tributary. In 1575, Paulo Dias had founded the colony of Angola on the East coast.

In all these countries and in many others the missionary accompanied the conqueror and trader, and in Abyssinia and Japan he had the foremost place. There the work was done by the Jesuits, while in India and Ceylon the Franciscans predominated at first and then the Jesuits, in East Africa and Indonesia the Dominicans. The missionary was a patriot as well as an evangelist, he inspired the soldier in sieges and battles, and, especially if he was a Jesuit, acted with success as diplomatic agent in the dealings of the State with Oriental rulers. The native converts were usually proud of their Portuguese connection and names and fought with the whites against its native and European foes. In Brazil the work of colonisation began in 1530, and the first governor went there in 1549. The limits of Portuguese rule had been confined to a strip of coast by the dividing line of Alexander VI, but a century later they were carried more than half way across the continent by the settlers. The first two hundred years of the history of Brazil is largely one of a struggle by the Jesuits to protect the native Indians from the rapacity of the colonists in search of labour and the problem was only settled by the importation of negro slaves from Africa to work the sugar estates. The latter were the chief source of wealth previous to the finding of gold and diamonds. At the present day, Brazil with its population of forty-five millions is a monument to the colonising capacity and enterprise of the Portuguese race.

The Portuguese went to India to look for spices and Christians (Henry had sought for a prince of his faith who would help him against Islam) but they had many disappointments before they found the Christians of St. Thomas, i.e., the descendants of those converted by the Apostle. Vasco da Gama and his companions were taken to a Hindu temple in Calicut and mistook it for a church, while King Manoel informed the Spanish sovereigns that the Indians were Christians but needed further instruction ; accordingly, a body of Franciscans went out with Cabral to establish a convent at Calicut and were involved in the attack on the factory. The early missionaries were too few to do more than attend to the needs of the soldiers and missionary enterprise did not really begin until the reign of John III and its great successes date from the arrival of St. Francis Xavier. Churches, schools, seminaries and convents were built and natives who embraced the Christian faith became in fact and not only in theory the equals of their white brethren, since they were equally eligible for many government posts.

The vast majority of Christians in India and Ceylon to-day descend from the natives baptised by the Portuguese and if the Catholic Church in Abyssinia founded by the Jesuits was submerged by a wave of nationalism, that country owes its separate existence and possession of any Christianity at all to the expedition of D. Christovăo da Gama in 1541, for to quote the words of Gibbon, " Ethiopia was saved by 450 Portuguese."

The results of Portuguese expansion could not be, and were not, confined to herself, they affected in a greater or less degree Western and Central Europe and large parts of Asia and Africa. The most important of these results, spiritual as well as material, sprang from the opening of the sea route to India round the Cape of Good Hope. This achievement, the result of the efforts of three generations of Portuguese sailors, restored the direct connection between Europe and the East which had been suspended for centuries in consequence of the territorial conquests of Islam. Henceforth, for 370 years, until the opening in our time of the Suez Canal, the main stream of trade between East and West was to flow round the South of Africa ; the Mediterranean lost its old importance in favour of the Atlantic and the face of Europe was turned in an opposite direction. From that date the commercial supremacy of Venice disappeared, while Lisbon and Antwerp, owing to its Portuguese factory, became the marts of Eastern products ; the drop in the price of drugs and spices benefited almost every European country, though the chief gain fell to the Portuguese crown which possessed a practical monopoly on them. This gain was shared by the great mercantile firms, both Italian and German, who hastened to set up agencies in Lisbon and at first were allowed to despatch private ships with the annual fleets. In the early years after the discovery, the profits were enormous and they enabled the Portuguese to secure their hold on Brazil, where for a lengthy period the expenses exceeded the returns. But so lucrative a trade could not always remain in the hands of a small power and when Portugal was conquered by Philip II in 1580, and that monarch closed the port of Lisbon to Dutch merchants, they and the English began to sail to the East and before the end of the century they overthrew the monopoly which the Portuguese had wrested from the Arabs.

The opening of the Cape route was only a part of the achievement of Portugal ; she showed the way through the seas of half the world and her pilots and charts taught her rivals to follow, but the merchantmen of Holland and England did not limit themselves to ploughing the Indian ocean. The English had already developed a trade with Morocco and sailed to Guinea for gold dust and slaves, while in the seventeenth century the Dutch captured the Portuguese settlements on the coast of West Africa as well as most of those in Asia ; in Brazil they seized Pernambuco and a large stretch of the coast line, but their attacks on Mozambique and Macau failed.

After the Restoration of 1640, the Portuguese recovered Brazil and Angola, but they had lost their hold on the East once and for all and the maritime supremacy of its seas had passed to the Northern Powers.

The benefits which accrued to Portugal from her expansion have been questioned by some publicists, and the net results of the policy are still in dispute among them.[1] It is agreed that she acquired considerable wealth from the East,[2] but the prosperity which followed from this source proved to be largely ephemeral. It was one thing to wrest a monopoly from the Arabs and Venetians by force of arms and

---

[1] They have been discussed by Dr. Mario de Albuquerque in a recent book, *O significado das navegações*, which he was good enough to send me. Its perusal led to the composition of this lecture.

[2] Besides spices and drugs, the imports included jewels, silks, porcelains and a host of other precious things. Pepper, however, was the most valuable commodity and Duarte Pacheco, writing about 1506, says that 30,000 or 40,000 quintals were yearly brought to Portugal (*Esmeraldo*, bk. 4, cap. 3). For the pepper trade, v, J. L. de Azevedo, *Epocas de Portugal Economico*, Lisbon, 1929, cap. 3. At first, pepper cost 2 cruzados the quintal at Cochin and fetched 30 in Lisbon.

another to carry on a vast commercial undertaking with success and add to it a political dominion which rarely paid its way. The Portuguese did not possess the business experience of their rivals, nor did King Manoel put up the capital required, hence Albuquerque had to complain that he was not supplied with enough silver to purchase spices or merchandise to give in exchange. Instead of providing a reserve fund, the King spent lavishly in pensions, embassies and buildings ; the equipment of fleets and the substitution of wrecked ships cost a large sum ; the fortresses in Morocco entailed a heavy loss and the capture of vessels by French corsairs impoverished the sovereign as well as his subjects, since by 1534 no fewer than 350 had been seized.[1] The spices alone sold in the India House in Lisbon during the twenty-four years of his reign produced a sum equal to 67,845 contos[2] or £15,000,000 in our pre-war money. In addition, large quantities were disposed of by the Treasury to Italian bankers and in the Portuguese factories abroad, yet in 1544 John III could not meet his engagements and the money he owed doubled every four years.[3]

Few will deny the glory that Portugal acquired by the discoveries and conquests of her sailors and soldiers, the apostolic labours and scientific work of her missionaries and the diffusion of her language, which became a *lingua franca* and has left words in scores of Asiatic tongues. Nevertheless, many writers and especially nineteenth century Liberals like Rebello da Silva[4] and Oliveira Martins, have condemned the Eastern venture, and the latter represents it as rash in conception, immoral in execution and ruinous in its

[1]Frei Luis de Sousa, *Annays de D. João III*, p. 381.
[2]Braamcamp Freire in *Archivo Historico Portuguez*, vol. 6, p. 375.
[3]Frei Luis de Sousa, *op. cit.*, p. 417.
[4]*Historia de Portugal nos seculos XVII e XVIII*, bk. 6, cap. 1.

results.[1]   On the other hand, though Brazil ultimately absorbed more men and capital than India, its conquest escaped censure because in addition to giving sugar, dyewood, gold and diamonds, it afforded a field for emigration and the propagation of the Faith, while the advantages derived from the possession of the Atlantic islands have been universally admitted.

Luis Mendes de Vasconcellos, who had been Captain-Major in the East and was to govern Angola, treats the question from various points of view in the dialogues of his work *O Sitio de Lisboa*, published in 1608.   His argument is as follows.   Lisbon has grown as a result of the voyages,[2] but India robs the country of labourers and soldiers and those who speculate in such matters say that there are now many waste lands which were once cultivated.   But if this is not true, we should have had less of them if, instead of putting their hopes on the East, men had occupied themselves with what they had at home.   Many who go out remain there and those who return, being either rich or old, serve for little.   He overlooks the fact that some at least must have employed the capital they brought back.   He does not deny that large profits have been made out of the India trade, but he laments the fact that it takes silver from Portugal, that is to pay for goods, and only gives carpets, by which he evidently means luxuries, in exchange.

Though a soldier, he considers the foundation of settlements in the East to have been an error on account of their distance from home and the cost of their defence, but at the same time declares that those who made them, "navigating so many seas and fighting

[1] *Historia de Portugal*, vol. 1.

[2] He says that as many as 200 merchant vessels are known to have entered the port in one tide and that 100, 70 and 50 were common numbers. *Op. cit.*, ed. Lisbon, 1786, p. 217.

with so many and such varied nations achieved, a work worthy of eternal remembrance." [1]

When Luis Mendes wrote, the Portuguese had been in the East for a little more than a century and though the Golden Age had passed and they had recently lost their trading monopoly, they still preserved their political power almost intact. But this last had suffered a total eclipse by 1655, when the learned Manoel Severim de Faria published his *Noticias de Portugal;* the fortresses of Ormuz and Malacca and nearly all of Ceylon had passed into other hands, while Goa itself had been blockaded more than once for many months by Dutch fleets. Under these altered circumstances it is interesting to compare his opinions with those of Luis Mendes which they much resemble. He begins by stating that the population of Portugal increased, not only in the Middle Ages, but even more in the fifteenth century and that after the discovery of India it began to diminish, and now he says : " we find a lack of men for war and navigation and more especially for the cultivation of the soil and in the absence of Portuguese, most farmers use Guinea slaves and mulattoes."

Coming next to the causes of the shortage, he attributes it to the colonies in general, which, though useful for the propagation of the Gospel and for trade, had robbed Portugal of men. He, however considers, those on this side of the Cape, that is the Atlantic islands, Angola and Brazil less prejudicial because they claim fewer men, but condemns the settlements beyond it on the ground that they absorb many soldiers and are very costly. He refers with approval to the words of D. Francisco de Almeida to King Manoel, " the more fortresses you have, the weaker you will be, let all your force be on the sea for if we are

[1] *Op. cit.*, pp. 63-78.

not powerful there, all will be against us." [1]   This point of view found many supporters in the Royal Council, so that after his final capture of Goa, Albuquerque in a letter to that monarch claimed more credit for defending the city from the Portuguese who wished to abandon it than for taking it twice from the Moors.

His policy prevailed and though the Portuguese had only gone to the East for trade, like the Dutch and English, circumstances obliged them to be conquerors and rulers.   No doubt it would have been better if they could have limited their responsibilities to a few strongholds on land, supplemented by factories and naval squadrons to guard them and the trade routes, but experience showed that unprotected factories were sure to be attacked and the possession of at least one strip of territory of their own, such as Goa, could not be dispensed with.   Fortresses in the towns of native rulers were not sufficient, for in the event of a serious reverse at sea, they would be besieged and could hold out for a time but not indefinitely.   Albuquerque was right in contending that a dominion founded on a navy alone could not last, for sailing ships had to stay in port during the monsoon, so that for some months in the year command of the sea and therefore support for the garrisons on shore was lacking.[2]

Severim was a priest and a Canon of Evora Cathedral and though he did not agree with the policy of expansion, he believed that his countrymen were the unconscious instruments of Providence in pursuing it. Even now, many will agree with him.   " God, who wished to spread the Faith in those parts, ordained that the Kings and their advisers should approve the conquest and by evident miracles the Portuguese

[1]Gaspar Correa, *Lendas da India*, vol. I, p. 906.

[2]*Cartas*, vol. I, pp. 98, 411, 419-422, 427.

185

became almost lords of all the Eastern seas and the chief ports of their coasts, gaining immortal fame by their achievements and preaching the holy Gospel, to the great glory of God and the profit of numberless souls who were baptised."

The ill results attributed by these political thinkers to the Eastern dominion may be classified under three heads :

1. The decay of agriculture and industry in Portugal.

2. A decline in her population.

3. The demoralisation of the conquerors, which infected the mother country.

Let us examine these charges and first look at the condition of agriculture and industry before the ocean voyages began. There is ample evidence to show that by far the greater part of the land was uncultivated and the industries rudimentary ; and until well into the eighteenth century similar conditions prevailed. The country did not produce corn enough to feed the population in a normal year, and it was necessary to make up the shortage from abroad. The *Lei das Sesmarias* of King Fernando was decreed to supply a then existing deficit, but it failed in its purpose and the reference to an age of abundance can only be taken to describe with truth the remote period of Moorish domination before the wars of reconquest. In fact, Portugal by its climate is not naturally one of the corn producing countries, though it is eminently suited for wine, fruits and oil.[1]

When the voyages were already in progress, about 1536, Garcia de Resende bore witness to a remarkable

[1]Costa Lobo, *Historia da Sociedade em Portugal no seculo XV*, Lisbon, 1903, p. 530, *et seq.*, A. G. Ramalho, *Legislação Agricola*, Lisbon, 1905, vol. 1, p. 182 and vol. 2, p. 114.

activity in bringing further land under cultivation[1] ;
he says that he saw woodland broken up and marshes
drained and it is reasonable to suppose that the profits
of the India trade paid part of the expenses. His
testimony is confirmed by the Count da Castanheira,
Overseer of Finance to John III, who tells us that the
King spent large sums in making marsh lands fit to
grow corn,[2] moreover in this reign the introduction
of maize came to compensate in part for the shortage
in other breadstuffs, while the production of fruits and
oil increased and wine found a market in India and
Brazil. In his *Descripção de Portugal,* written half a
century later, the historian and lawyer Duarte Nunes
de Leão devotes some chapters to a eulogy of the riches
of the soil. He makes only a passing reference to years
when corn was scarce, and insinuates that the peasants
were then content with fish, fruits, meat and vegetables
as substitutes. He also says that in the " last few
years " owing to bumper crops it was possible to send
bread to Spain. But the information we possess as
to the state of agriculture in the sixteenth and
seventeenth centuries is contradictory and the view we
take will depend to some extent on our conclusions as
to the population, which tended to be regulated by
the means of subsistence. As regards industry, the
colonial expansion led to the creation of new under-
takings, such as shipbuilding and rope making, the
manufacture of damask and leather work, sweetmeats
and preserved fruits, the last two of which were
exported. It must be admitted, however, that some
of these industries served only for ostentation and
were luxuries rather than necessities.

Other writers have followed Severim de Faria in
stating that the population of Portugal went down in

[1]*Miscelanea,* ed. Coimbra, 1798, p. 370.
[2]Frei Luis de Sousa, *op. cit.,* p. 405.

187

the sixteenth century, but without supplying elements of proof ; unfortunately only one national census was then taken, that of 1527-1530, from which, with Costa Lobo, we may reasonably fix the number of inhabitants at 1,122,112.

It is true that Evora shrank when the Court removed to Lisbon, but Costa Lobo shows that not only the capital, but Oporto and other towns grew in size.[1] They doubtless did so at the expense of the provinces, but this happened in other lands. The alleged decrease is usually attributed to the drain of men to the East, and the many severe plagues,[2] which afflicted the country are often left out of the reckoning, but if a decline took place, it is difficult to see how the annual fleets to India could have been despatched, not to speak of those to Brazil, and how the garrisons in the fortresses in Morocco, which were engaged in almost continual warfare with the Moors, could have been kept up to strength. In the course of the century following the first voyage of Vasco da Gama at least 200,000 men sailed to the East ; the figure includes those who went more than once, but only a small proportion returned. Of the rest some died at sea or in battle, others married and reared families in the Portuguese settlements, others again entered the service of native rulers or created trading communities in their territories, like those of Hoogli in Bengal, Siriam in Pegu, Timor in the Sunda islands and Macau in China. These were independent of the Viceroys, though the last two afterwards became colonies and they still fly the Portuguese flag. Trading usually involved fighting and from this cause and from shipwreck, climate, lack of hygiene and medical help

[1]*Op. cit.*, cap. 1.

[2]In the sixteenth century there were epidemics of plague in 1502, 1506, 1513, 1521, 1569, 1581 and 1578-1579.

the death rate must have been enormous. Diogo do Couto estimates the number of his countrymen in the East as 16,000 at the end of the sixteenth century,[1] that is only four times as many as in the first quarter, but a large proportion of the others were certainly absorbed in the native stocks, so that their descendents inherited nothing European except at times the name.

In discussing the effects of the voyages Costa Lobo points out that emigration does not necessarily lead to a decline in numbers at home and he quotes the following instances : from 1801 to 1835 Portugal was devastated by three foreign invasions and suffered revolutionary outbreaks, a civil war, and an epidemic of cholera, but the population grew ; again, between 1878 and 1890 no fewer than 260,000 persons left the country for Brazil and yet at the close of the same period there were half a million more inhabitants.[2]

The alleged decline has also been charged in part to the decrees of John II and Manuel I for the expulsion of the Jews and Moors, but the fact that they were not carried out to the letter is forgotten. The overwhelming majority of the Jews accepted baptism and remained, though when the Inquisition got to work and apostasy met with severe punishment, many of these slunk away to foreign parts. The Moors who still practised their religion consisted only of a few communities and the number that emigrated seems to have been insignificant.[3]

Almost the only piece of evidence cited to support the theory of a fall in the total numbers is the inadequate force which King Sebastian was able to collect

[1]*Soldado Pratico*, pt. 2, p. 33. Half castes born in India are no doubt included in the number.

[2]*Op. cit.*, p. 58.

[3]Costa Lobo, *op. cit.*, pp. 33-48, *cf.* Santarem, *Memorias das Cortes Geraes*, I, pp. 44 and 59 (reprinted ed.).

in 1578, but the unpopularity of the African expedition would go far to explain it. If we accept as correct the figure of 1,200,000 for the population in 1639, deduced by Rebello da Silva,[1] it would seem that it remained stationary, the natural increase being nullified by plagues and the drain of men to the colonies.

We have seen that, according to Severim de Faria, the places of those who went to the East were taken by slaves, and it is a fact that these were employed in agriculture and that by their labour they increased the cultivated area, while others discharged the menial offices in the capital. In the sixteenth century the population of Lisbon was variously estimated by contemporaries as from 52,000 in 1527, to 98,000 in 1551, rising in 1620 to 126,000, and the number of slaves as a tenth—but this last is little more than guesswork.[2] From recent research we learn that in the last quarter of the fifteenth century the average importation did not exceed 500, but the figure grew to 10,000 in the sixteenth, though a large proportion of them did not stay in Portugal but were sent into Spain or to South America. Public opinion welcomed their introduction, but they prejudiced free labour and fostered habits of indolence among the Portuguese ; Nunes de Leão, optimist though he usually is, confesses that his people are averse to manual work and that, to get rich quickly, they embrace the ocean voyages as less laborious though more perilous.[3]

The common allegation that the East corrupted its conquerors would be more convincing if we had reason to think that they were the pick of their nation and

[1]*Op. cit.*, vol. 4, p. 421.

[2]Writing about 1536, Cleynarts, the Belgian humanist, and Garcia de Resende greatly exaggerate the slave population. *Nic Clenardi Epistolarum*, ed. Hanover, 1606, p. 60 ; Resende, *Miscelanea*, ed. 1798, p. 363.

[3]*Op. cit.*, p. 64.

could put entire faith in contemporary historians ; Gaspar Correa, Diogo do Couto, and João Ribeiro blazon forth the misdeeds of their compatriots and Rodrigues Silveira, an old soldier with grievances, has rarely a word to say in their defence in his *Memorias do um Soldado da India.*[1] We know, however, that a large proportion of those who embarked were convicts, vagrants and adventurers, men who were shy of work and not wanted at home, but who were quite willing to fight.[2] Further as time went on, the crews must have contained more and more cornermen and country louts who could not tell the difference between larboard and starboard, though the six months' voyage round the Cape gave such improvised sailors time enough to become perfect salts. The letters from the Town Council of Goa to the King in the last decade of the sixteenth century also contain frequent complaints of the Viceroys and give the impression that the military position was desperate,[3] but if conditions were as bad as they assert, it is hard to understand how in a perennial condition of war the State continued to hold most of the fortresses and settlements for another fifty years.[4]

Historians are generally agreed that abuse of power, extortion and piracy, while rare at first, had become common long before the end of the sixteenth century. Diogo do Couto dates the moral decay from the time following the rule of D. Constantino de Braganza, that is from 1561, nevertheless it did not impair military

[1]Lisbon, 1877, edited by Costa Lobo from Add. MS. 25419, British Museum.

[2]Barros, *Asia*, Dec. 1, bk. 1, cap. 1. Couto, *Asia*, Dec. 5, bk. 3, cap. 8.

[3]*Archivo Portuguez Oriental*, fasc. 1, 2nd ed., Nova Goa, 1877.

[4]These are depicted in colour and described in detail in the MS. work of Barreto de Resende, *Livro do estado da India Oriental*, (1634) of which the British Museum has a copy, Sloane MS. 197. The Viceroy's portraits are included.

qualities, for ten years later under D. Luis de Ataide, a great figure, the few thousands of Portuguese in India were able to repel the attacks of a powerful league of native princes who sought to expel them.[1]

It is no doubt true that some of his successors paid little attention to the orders of the King and to the interests of those they ruled ; they apparently thought first of enriching themselves and military and civilian officials naturally followed in their train, but the temptations were very great for poor men, and neither the Dutch nor the English resisted these much better. The absolute power of the Viceroy, the immunity of a fidalgo from punishment, the sale of posts, the distance between India and Portugal and the unique chance of making a fortune help to explain many of the mis-demeanours and the milieu contributed to them, for it is alleged that even honest characters lost their scruples when they passed the Cape of Good Hope. The main cause, however, in the opinion of Cardinal Cerejeira,[2] lay in the Portuguese themselves, and yet as regards the Viceroys, it is right to state that very few of their letters to the Kings have been printed, so that we are bound to suspend judgment until we can read their defence. In the meantime we can safely discount a proportion of the charges, owing to the Portuguese habits of exaggeration and *mal dizer*. Moreover, completely disinterested and noble characters were found among all classes, some of whom are generally known, like D. John de Castro and Antonio Galvão, while humbler names are registered in the rare book

---

[1] As late, however, as the eighteenth century the rule of the East India Company was associated with greed and extortion by some critics, and Horace Walpole could say, " We are Spaniards in our lust for gold and Dutch in our delicacy of obtaining it."

[2] *Clenardo*, Coimbra, 1926, cap. 3.

Primor e honra da vida soldadesca no Estado da India[1]
and elsewhere. These and many others rose to their
responsibilities, both as Christians and as subjects of
the four Kings who ruled Portugal in the sixteenth
century, all of whom compare most favourably with
sovereigns of the time elsewhere.

However corrupt many of the Portuguese in the
East may have been, they often evinced remarkable
solidarity and patriotism. The municipality of Goa
repeatedly lent large sums of money to the Viceroys
for the equipment of military expeditions to distant
parts of the wide-flung dominion of the State, though
repayment, if made at all, came many years later. The
inhabitants of one settlement would assist those of
another in time of danger with men and arms without
hope of reward.

Albuquerque warned King Manuel that India had
to be held by force, but the Portuguese were only a
handful compared with the hundreds of thousands of
their actual and potential foes, who possessed im-
measurably greater resources ; the Viceroys hardly ever
disposed of men and money sufficient for defence or
attack, and the Kings of Portugal, having many other
commitments, did not and usually could not supply
them. The principal receipts of the various fortresses
were regarded as the perquisites of their Captains,
who were permitted to make fortunes as a reward for
their military services past and present, or those of their
forbears, while the State remained poor, and yet but
for the public spirit and the valour of these Captains,
of common soldiers and even of traders in many an
emergency, the flag could not have been kept flying so
long as it was.

It is a curious fact that, along with the increasing

[1]Lisbon, 1630. The author is unknown but he wrote his book during
the reign of King Sebastian.

lack of scruple among governors and officials, went a spiritual and moral revival, mainly due to the Jesuits, both at home and in the East; but as in Portugal this revival came too late to prevent the defeat at Alcacer and the loss of independence, which was generally attributed to the sins of the nation, so in India it could not save Portuguese supremacy. This was doomed when the Dutch obtained the command of the sea on which the State depended. Yet Antonio Bocarro, last of the great chroniclers of India, writing in 1631, could take pride in the fact that his countrymen were fighting with their backs to the wall against native and European foes to maintain the standard of the Cross and no longer for worldly gain, since their trade had been by then almost entirely extinguished.

Those who left Lisbon for the East during the first three quarters of the sixteenth century had a fair prospect of reaching their destination, but the men who went out between 1580 and 1612 must have had the reckless daring of the gambler ; from 1497 to 1579 no fewer than 620 vessels sailed from Portugal for India of which only 31 were wrecked, while in the later period of thirty years the losses among 186 vessels rose to 35.[1]

Owing to the conditions of life at sea it sometimes happened that nearly half the soldiers on board died of sickness, usually dysentery or scurvy,[2] while many of the others had to enter hospital as soon as they landed. The large proportion of wrecks in the time of Philip II was mainly due to cupidity; the vessels were too large to be manageable, some went to the bottom owing to the bad condition of their timbers, or through being

[1]L. de Figueiredo Falcão, *Livro em que se contem toda a fazenda dos reinos de Portugal India e Ilhas*, Lisbon, 1859, p. 194.

[2]Couto, *op. cit.*, Dec. 9, cap. 11, and see the accounts of travellers such as Mocquet, Pyrard, Sassetti and Pawlowski.

overladen,[1] while others ran on shore by reason of the ignorance or carelessness of the pilots and thus they earned a place in that prose epic of rare literary and historical value the *Historia Tragico-Maritima*.[2]

What reader can quite forget those graphic and moving stories ? Some tell of the tramp of hundreds of men and a few women also, month after month through wild, trackless and unknown country from the neighbourhood of the Cape to Delagoa Bay and even to Sofala ; the daily fight for food, the struggle with fatigue and the cunning of the savage tribes, followed not rarely by death at their hands, or more commonly from exhaustion, and lastly the final victory of a small and hardy remnant in its return to civilisation. Ludovico di Varthema, who had lived with the Portuguese in India, said that he had never met braver men, and we can believe him.

The last question to be examined is the effect of the Eastern conquests on the character, not of a certain number of individuals in Portugal more or less connected with them, but on the people as a whole. In the absence of newspapers and the lack of epistolary correspondence of the period, any opinion we form

---

[1]Under King Manoel the India ships rarely exceeded 400 tons burden, but in the reign of John III their size was increased to 800 and 900, with the result that wrecks became more frequent and in 1570 a decree of King Sebastian restricted the size to 450 tons. Under Philip II the pepper trade, which continued to be a royal monopoly, and the building of the vessels to carry it on, were farmed to contractors who, to reduce expenses and increase profits, reverted to the larger type, and the wrecks attained a record figure. After 1622, representations led to the construction of smaller vessels which proved satisfactory. The Dutch used ships of about 500 tons and rarely lost them through any fault of theirs. Severim de Faria, *op. cit.*, p. 241, cf. Lucena, *Vida do Pe Francisco Xavier*, ed. 1600, bk. I, cap. 11, p. 41. Writing however in 1542 about the India ships, the Count da Castanheira asserts that in the last twenty-four years not a fourth as many have been lost as formerly. Frei Luis de Sousa, *op. cit.*, p. 405. For other causes of wrecks, see Lavanha, *Relação do naufragio da nao Santo Alberto* in *Historia Tragico-Maritima*, II, p. 226.

[2] 2 Vols., Lisbon, 1735-1736.

must be tentative, but it would seem that at first an increase in the national pride and sloth[1] followed by a wave of pessimism, were the most deleterious results. Both idealism and valour marked the nobles and squires who followed and died with King Sebastian in 1578, and if, in the East, Oriental luxury and immorality were rampant, in Portugal the former did not go beyond ostentation nor did the latter include the unnatural vices found in the Courts of the Italian States and France, which were a mark of the Renaissance.[2] Moreover, even in the East, the men who defended Goa and Chaul in 1570, who drove off the Achinese and Dutch from Malacca on many occasions and who in 1655-1656 held Colombo until they were reduced to a handful, could not have been degenerate. The six months' voyage to or from the East served in itself as a test of endurance such as we can hardly realise to-day. The Venerable Gonçalo da Silveira, proto-martyr of South Africa, says of it : "As death cannot well be described except by one who has attended a death bed, so the voyage from Portugal to India can only be related, or even believed, by him who has had that experience."[3]

The opposition to the Eastern adventure, which was voiced at the Royal Council in November, 1495, was undoubtedly prudent, and had the critics persuaded

[1] The disinclination to servile work which Duarte Nunes de Leão confesses and the "mania das grandezas" are stressed by most foreign travellers in Portugal in the sixteenth century. The poor gentleman who had little to eat at home, but walked through the streets attended by several servants whom he could not afford to pay is a type common in the plays of Gil Vicente. The men of that age cared not for comfort, but ostentation was the breath of their nostrils.

[2] According to the *Summario* of Christovam Roiz de Oliveira, the city of Lisbon about 1551 had 430 goldsmiths, 150 singers and 14 dancing academies but only 34 masters who taught the art of reading.

[3] *Diversi Avisi . . . dall' Indie di Portogallo ricevuti dall' anno* 1551, *fino al* 1558, etc., fol. 283.

King Manoel, it would have been to the spiritual and material advantage of countless Portuguese, but in that case the Christian faith would not have penetrated into India, Ceylon, and Japan and the neighbouring countries so early and with such success, and the army of converts and martyrs would have been far smaller. The history of Portugal would have been bereft of many of its outstanding figures and of its great poet, while some of its foremost prose writers would have lost their opportunity to enrich the literature ; Afonso de Albuquerque, Duarte Pacheco and scores of other soldiers and sailors would not have made their names illustrious. Mendes Pinto could not have produced his enthralling tale of travel, the *Peregrination,* nor Camoens his epic, *The Lusiads.* And lastly, we should have been deprived of the missionary records of heroic suffering and achievement which were rendered possible by the fact of Portuguese expansion. Portugal would still have deserved to rank as one of the most enterprising of nations, whether great or small, but she would have missed the high place she now occupies in world history.

By the mouths of the Old Man of Belem and the giant Adamastor, guardian of the Cape of Storms, Camoens condemns

> " the foolish lust
> For this mere vanity, which we call fame,"

and yet while after seventeen years of fighting and suffering he returned from the East a poor and broken man, he was proud to celebrate in song :

> " The arms and heroes signalised in fame,
> Who from the Western Lusitanian shore,
> Beyond e'en Taprobana, sailing came
> O'er seas uncrossed by any man before."

Though he does not hesitate to censure their misdeeds, his poem is a pæan to the *conquistadores,* but D. John de Castro, notwithstanding his profession of soldier and scientist, saw the great adventure from another plane and, in a letter to John III, he goes so far as to say: " More souls are lost among the Portuguese who come to India than saved of the heathen that our preachers convert to the Holy Faith."